FRESH THAI

OI CHEEPCHAIISSARA

METRO BOOKS
NEW YORK

To my parents, who provided all the good things
in life, including wonderful food for our family

Copyright © Octopus Publishing Group Ltd 2006

This 2008 edition published by Metro Books, by
arrangement with Hamlyn, a division of
Octopus Publishing Group Ltd.

Metro Books
122 Fifth Avenue
New York
NY10011

ISBN-13: 978-1-4351-0071-8
ISBN-10: 1-4351-0071-9

A catalogue record for this book is available from the
British Library

Printed and bound in China

1   3   5   7   9   10   8   6   4   2

Note

The Food and Drug Administration advises that eggs should not be
consumed raw. This book contains dishes made with raw or lightly
cooked eggs. It is prudent for vulnerable people such as pregnant and
nursing mothers, those with compromised immune systems, the
elderly, babies, and young children to avoid uncooked or lightly
cooked dishes made with eggs. Once prepared, these dishes should be
kept refrigerated and used promptly.

This book includes dishes made with nuts and nut derivatives. It is
advisable for those with known allergic reactions to nuts and nut
derivatives and those who may be potentially vulnerable to these
allergies, such as pregnant and nursing mothers, those with compromised
immune systems, the elderly, babies, and children to avoid dishes
made with nuts and nut oils. It is also prudent to check the labels of
pre-packaged ingredients for the possible inclusion of nut derivatives.

Ovens should be preheated to the specified temperature—if using a
convection oven, follow the manufacturer's instructions for adjusting
the time and the temperature.

Contents

Introduction

In Thailand we are passionate about our food. When my family gets together, my aunts and cousins usually bring their favorite dishes to add to an already sumptuous spread provided by the host. This often results in a surfeit of food—but nobody minds. We eat it gradually throughout the day, safe in the knowledge that there will be no adverse effects.

Our tendency to indulge in good food without putting on weight has attracted the attention of visitors from other countries. How do we do it, they wonder? There is no simple answer. Our intensely hot climate sometimes makes us sweat and expel excess salt, yet air-conditioning is widely used in homes, offices, and cars. We enjoy sports, but I doubt if we get more exercise than anyone else. So it must be the food. It is surely the freshness of Thai food—our love of fruits and vegetables straight from the market, delicious seafood straight from the sea, and, above all, fresh herbs rather than powdered spices—that makes our cuisine beneficial to everyone who eats it.

Cooking in the Thai style

Learning to cook Thai, if you are not yourself Thai, is perfectly feasible—and great fun. Our cuisine is not vast, but it is certainly varied, with influences from China, India, and the Muslim countries to the south. If you think Thai, you will soon find yourself thinking about coconut, ginger, lemongrass, garlic, galangal, cilantro, fish sauce, hot chilies, and jasmine rice.

The Thai style of cooking is different from the Western approach. In this book I bridge the gap by providing tested measurements that will enable you to obtain excellent results if you follow the directions precisely. However, Thai cooks tend to rely on tasting rather than measurement. From long experience they can tell exactly when a dish has that unique combination of ingredients that makes it authentic. To reach that level of expertise you will need to get into the spirit of Thai cooking, and with that in mind I offer the following advice.

Try to achieve a balanced taste, both in individual dishes and in the meal as a whole. Underlying Thai cuisine are the five flavors: sweet, sour, salty, bitter, and hot. We derive sweetness from palm sugar, cane sugar, and from sweet fruits, such as pineapples; sourness comes from lime, lemon, and vinegar; saltiness comes from fish sauce and shrimp paste; bitter melon provides the bitter taste that is occasionally introduced into the larger meals; and heat comes from both fresh and dried chilies. Combine these flavors in a harmonious way—not necessarily in equal proportions—and you are beginning to cook in the Thai spirit.

Presentation is an integral part of Thai cooking, and the food must appeal to the eye as well as the palate. Here we are dealing with colors, shapes, and textures, using garnishes such as finely sliced red chilies to contrast with the green of the cilantro or the whiteness of the rice. There is no need to prepare elaborate fruit and vegetable carvings, which adorn the tables at weddings and other feasts, but it is easy to learn how to make a few deft cuts in a long chili and watch it splay out into a beautiful flower shape when you place it in a bowl of water. With a few touches like that, your home-prepared meal will look and taste authentically Thai.

Achieving authenticity

In the cooking classes that I have run for several years, I always introduce people to dishes that really are authentic, just like those you can eat in Thailand. I am not entirely against adaptation, however. It is sometimes necessary, because finding authentic ingredients for a particular dish may be difficult. It can be quite acceptable—even preferable—to substitute a locally grown, fresh vegetable for an imported Thai vegetable and still retain an authentic Thai flavor from the herbs and sauces.

There is no need to be too rigid in attempting to use fresh herbs and vegetables on every occasion. For example, dried chilies are an essential

ingredient in Thai cooking, and they impart a stronger flavor and aroma than fresh chilies. It is worth remembering that some frozen vegetables (peas are a good example) can actually be more nutritious than their market-fresh equivalents. You will still get acceptable results if you buy plenty of lemongrass, ginger, and other vital ingredients and store them in the freezer. You can also keep the labor-intensive curry pastes in the freezer for several weeks, using them as they are needed.

Cooking for health
For this book I have made some minor adaptations to my traditional recipes in order to enhance their benefits to health. You will notice that there are no deep-fried dishes. I have also reduced the amount of salt while making sure that the food still tastes delicious. In many of the stir-fry dishes, I have used sunflower oil, which is popular in Thailand. I use a nonstick wok rather than an iron wok, and I urge you to do the same. In that way you can cook successfully with just a tiny amount of oil, keeping all the fats to a minimum.

In Thailand there is a large industry that processes coconuts to make coconut cream (from the first pressing) and coconut milk. In rich food coconut cream is delicious, but here I have kept a good flavor by using a half-measure of coconut milk (with its lower fat content) together with a half-measure of either stock—such as chicken stock for chicken curry—or water. The result, I hope you will agree, is very acceptable—and with luck it will help you live longer to enjoy more good food.

Regional variations
The recipes in this book are based on dishes from all the regions of Thailand, but mostly from the central plain, which is dominated by Bangkok, and the southern peninsula. This is because I was born in the south, in Hat Yai, but went to college in Bangkok, where I later worked. I have traveled to the other regions, frequently to the mountainous north but also to the dry land to the east. Each region has a distinctive cuisine, but they all tend to get mixed up in the vast metropolis of Bangkok.

In the north, people enjoy milder curries, glutinous (sticky) rice, and specialties such as spicy pork sausages. From the central plain come favorite dishes such as hot and sour soup; green curry; and chicken, coconut, and galangal soup. In the south we love hot curries—and the seafood is exceptional. I wish I could take you to my family's shrimp farm near Songkhla to grill jumbo shrimp with scallops and pineapple. We have built a house by the lake where we cook in the traditional manner and eat outdoors on a low table.

Serving Thai food
If you are going to cook Thai food at home it will be most effective if you follow Thai custom and serve all the dishes at the same time. Visitors are often surprised by this practice, expecting to start with a separate soup course, followed by fish and meat dishes. But having everything together, except dessert, is the only way to enjoy Thai food properly. You need to be able to dilute the powerful flavors of the soups with a spoonful of rice or share the special fish dishes among your guests.

To help you create some balanced Thai meals I have made some menu suggestions, but please add your favorite dishes if I have not included them. It is essential to have steamed rice and customary to have soup, a curry dish or a spicy salad, a vegetable dish, and a dipping sauce. In the south we nearly always have fish or seafood as an option, while dishes based on tofu are becoming increasingly popular, especially among vegetarians.

Although we eat plenty of fish and seafood and relatively small quantities of red meat, many people in Thailand are strict vegetarians. In their home cooking they substitute the usual fish sauce with soy sauce, or shrimp paste with soybean paste. It can require more imagination to make vegetarian dishes truly tasty, but Thai chili sauces and relishes are great in salads or mixed into stir-fries with tofu.

With so many starters, soups and main dishes, it may be surprising to find that we are fond of desserts in Thailand. Although not all of them appeal to Western taste, many do. For example, we have some delightful, cooling desserts. What could be better on a hot summer day than Watermelon Sorbet? Or, if the weather is colder, try Black Sticky Rice with Egg Custard, if you are not already *im* (full).

There are many traditions in Thai cooking but no fixed rules. Centuries ago we tried chilies brought to us by the Portuguese; now it is hard to imagine Thai cooking without them. Our cuisine is constantly evolving, and we love to try new tastes to see if they will harmonize. Now it is your turn to cook something fresh. It is time to start cooking Fresh Thai.

Pantry ingredients

Many of the ingredients used in the recipes in this book are available in large supermarkets, but some of them will be found only in Asian or specialty Thai shops. If there are no specialty retailers in your area, you can also purchase these ingredients on the Internet.

BEAN SAUCE Black bean sauce is made from fermented black beans and is used to add a salty taste to stir-fried meat, vegetables, or seafood. Yellow bean sauce, which also imparts saltiness, is made from yellow soybeans and is often added to chicken, pork, or vegetable stir-fries.

COCONUT MILK A low-fat version of coconut milk with 65 percent less fat than regular coconut milk is available, but my method of using a half-measure of regular coconut milk and either water or stock will give similar results.

CILANTRO ROOT The root of cilantro is used only in Thai cuisine, so its inclusion in a recipe makes a dish particularly authentic. The leaves are used as a garnish, but the roots are used in pastes and in any dish that needs the full flavor of cilantro. It can be found in both Thai and Asian supermarkets.

DRIED BLACK FUNGUS A popular ingredient in stir-fries and vegetarian dishes, dried black fungus, or cloud ears, are thin, ruffle-edged, black mushrooms. They are similar in appearance to wood ears

but are slightly smaller, lighter in color, and have a more delicate flavor. Use them to add a crunchy texture to a dish. Soften them in hot water for a few minutes before using them.

GROUND DRIED SHRIMP This ingredient, known as *kung haeng*, is the result of grinding dried shrimp until they become fluffy. It is widely used in traditional Thai cooking.

GROUND RICE This dry-fry rice is made by frying jasmine rice in a pan over medium heat. Put 2 tablespoons of uncooked jasmine rice in a small pan and fry for 6–8 minutes or until brown, shaking the pan continually to move the rice around in the pan. Use a mortar and pestle or a small blender to grind the rice to a powder. Keep it in an airtight jar and use it as needed.

KAFFIR LIME LEAVES Among the most important ingredients in Thai cuisine, kaffir lime leaves give their best flavor when they are fresh rather than dried or frozen. They are readily available outside Thailand in most large supermarkets.

KRACHAI Smaller and with a more intense flavor than ginger, fresh *krachai* or lesser ginger (as it is also called) can be bought in Thai and Asian supermarkets. It should be thinly peeled and finely sliced before use.

LEMONGRASS This is available in most supermarkets these days. The wonderful, lemony flavor comes from the white part, near the base of the stem.

NOODLES Noodles come in many different shapes and sizes, and can be either fresh or dried. Fresh noodles can be found in the refrigerated section of your Asian market. Dried noodles also come in bundles kept in plastic bags. Rice noodles are made from a paste of rice flour and water, which is steamed in large trays and then cut into different widths. *Sen yai* or wide noodles are about ¾ inch wide; *sen lek* are less than ¼ inch (5 mm) wide; and *sen mii* vermicelli are very thin indeed, just over 1⁄16 inch (1 mm) thick. Rice flake noodles (*kuay chap*) are big, flat noodles the size of tortilla chips. There are also non-rice noodles, such as wheat noodles (*ba mii*), which are made with egg; and mung bean starch noodles (*wun sen*), which, like *sen mii*, are sometimes called vermicelli. Most of the dried noodles need to be soaked in water at room temperature for 4–5 hours or overnight, which will prevent them from breaking up when they are cooked.

OIL Sunflower oil is high in polyunsaturates, which are believed to break down cholesterol. Sesame oil, which is made from roasted sesame seeds, can be used sparingly for its aroma and rich flavor.

PALM OR COCONUT SUGAR These sugars, which are available in jars or cake form, are used in Thai cooking because they are local products. Try to obtain them for an authentic flavor, but if you cannot find them use raw (turbinado) sugar instead.

PAPAYAS These fruits turn from green to yellow-orange as they ripen. In supermarkets they are often sold partially ripe, but you need to find a green one in a Thai or Asian supermarket for the classic dish of green papaya salad.

POMELO The pomelo is related to the grapefruit, which can be used as an alternative, but its skin is much thicker than that of an orange or grapefruit. To peel it, slice a circular patch off the top of the fruit, about ¼ inch (5 mm) deep (roughly the thickness of the skin). Then score five deep lines from top to bottom, dividing the skin into five segments. Now peel off the skin, one segment at a time. Remove any remaining pith and separate the segments of the fruit. Crumble the segments into their component parts, without squashing them or releasing the juice.

PRESERVED RADISH Known as *chai poh*, preserved radish is crunchy and spicy and has a touch of sweetness and saltiness. It is finely chopped and sold in vacuum packs and jars in Thai and Asian supermarkets.

SHREDDED COCONUT This is a useful ingredient to keep in the pantry. It can be spread on salads. Sweetened or unsweetened, it is available in packets from Thai and Asian supermarkets. If you want to remove the

sugar from sweetened coconut, soak it in a mixture of one part milk, one part water for an hour in the refrigerator. Drain it and pat dry, and it is ready for use.

THAI JASMINE RICE Rice is essential in Thai cooking and it is served at all meals. The best variety to use for Thai cuisine is jasmine rice, with its natural, delicate fragrance. Brown rice has plenty of vitamins and comes in smaller bags than jasmine rice. Bags of rice can be kept in the pantry for at least a year. White and black sticky rice are used for desserts, but accompaniments to some of the Thai dishes can also have a sticky texture.

THAI SWEET BASIL Often used for garnishing, Thai sweet basil (*bai horapha*) has purple stems and a unique taste and fragrance. Although you can use other types of basil with acceptable results, the dishes will not be completely authentic.

TOFU Available in soft, silky, and firm forms, tofu or beancurd can be bought fresh or in long-life packs. Soft tofu can be served with fresh herbs and dressing, in soup dishes, and for dessert. Firm tofu is used for stir-fries and is added to curry dishes.

WRAPPERS Spring roll sheets, filo pastry sheets (thawed before use), and fresh wonton sheets can be kept in the refrigerator for a few days. All of these wrappers can be kept in the freezer for at least 3 months.

Preparing seafood

Careful preparation will greatly improve your seafood dishes. In Thailand, food is quick to cook but takes time to prepare.

CRAB To remove the cool cooked crab meat from the shell, lay the crab on its back and twist off the legs and claws. Cover it with plastic wrap or a cloth and crack the legs and claws by tapping them with a rolling pin or a small hammer. Use a skewer or pick to remove the flesh. Discard the cartilage and membranes. Place the crab on its back, push up the apron with your thumbs, and separate it from the shell. Remove and discard the spongy gills, as the lungs are sometimes called. Use a skewer to pick out the white meat and place it in a bowl. Press down on the mouth of the shell to crack it away. Discard the cartilage, membrane, and stomach sac, all of which are found in the shell. Remove the soft brown meat. Crack the under-shell and remove it at the joint. Clean out the shell and use the white and dark meat, or shell, as required. Alternatively, ask your fishmonger to cook and shell crabs for you.

Live, uncooked crabs should be scrubbed and put in the freezer for 30 minutes to firm up the flesh. Twist off and remove the upper shell and discard the stomach sac and the soft gill tissue. Leaving the legs attached, cut the crab in half through the center of the shell from head to rear. Then cut it in half again from left to right, quartering the crab and leaving the legs attached to each quarter. Using a cracker or the back of a heavy knife, crack the crab claws to make them easier to eat.

FISH Whole flat fish, such as turbot, snapper, plaice, sea bream, and sea bass, should be cleaned and gutted but the head left on. Score with a sharp knife three or four times on both sides and dry thoroughly.

To prepare whole round fish, such as sea or freshwater trout, mackerel, and red or gray mullet, hold the fish firmly by the tail and, if necessary, scrape with a knife or a shell from tail to head to remove the excess scales. Trim the fins and cut the tail into a neat V with scissors. Lay the fish on a cutting board or waxed paper. With a sharp knife, slit the belly, scrape and discard the gut. Leave the head on if you wish. Clean and score with a sharp knife, making three or four slashes in each side. You can ask your fishmonger to prepare the fish for you if you are short on time.

MUSSELS AND CLAMS Clean and scrub mussels or clams with a stiff brush. Throw away any empty shells and any that are cracked or open. Use a small, sharp knife to scrape away the beard from the mussels. Wash both mussels and clams in several changes of cold water until the water is left clean. Put them in a large bowl, cover with cold water, and let stand for 30 minutes. Drain and set aside.

SHRIMP Use fresh, medium to large shrimp. Clean and pinch off the legs and head, then peel and devein the shrimp to remove the intestinal tract (the black line). Cut them open like a butterfly but leave the halves joined at the tails. You do not need to devein small shrimp.

SCALLOPS All my scallop recipes use both types of meat found in the shell: the white, meaty part and the coral, which is the bright orange roe. To prepare, grip the scallop in one hand using a hand towel, insert a knife or special tool, and twist open the shell. Remove the meat with a sharp knife and trim off the dark strings of intestinal tract.

SQUID Pull the body away from the head and tentacles. Open the tentacles, then press the hard part of the head so that the "beak" comes out. Discard it. Cut off the tentacles. Empty the squid pouches and pull off the purplish skin. Rinse the squid and tentacles thoroughly. Use the body for stuffing, cut it into rings, or cut it in half and open the body pouches. Lightly score the outside of each squid with a sharp knife, making diagonal cross cuts to form a diamond pattern, and cut into pieces about 1½ inches square.

Menu plans

MENU FOR 2 PEOPLE

Garlic shrimp

Red curry chicken with Thai baby eggplants
(use ½ quantity)

Boiled jasmine rice

Quail eggs in ginger syrup (use ½ quantity)

MENU FOR 2 PEOPLE

Stir-fried mushrooms with ginger

Green curry beef with bamboo shoots

Boiled jasmine rice

Watermelon sorbet

MENU FOR 2 PEOPLE

Spring-flowering chives with squid

Panaeng chicken curry (use ½ quantity)

Boiled jasmine rice

Sticky rice with mango (use ½ quantity)

FAMILY MENU FOR 4 PEOPLE

Barbecued pork spare ribs with honey

Steamed fish with chili and lime juice

Green curry beef with bamboo shoots

Stir-fried mushrooms with ginger

Boiled jasmine rice

Sticky rice with mango

FAMILY MENU FOR 4 PEOPLE

Broiled shrimp and scallops with pineapple

Stir-fried mixed vegetables

Panaeng chicken curry

Hot and sour soup with seafood

Boiled jasmine rice

Sago pudding with white lotus seeds

FAMILY SEAFOOD MENU FOR 4 PEOPLE

Pan-fried fishcakes with green beans served
with cucumber relish

Black sesame seeds with shrimp and water
chestnuts

Red curry with fish and tofu

Stir-fried mixed vegetables

Boiled jasmine rice

Quail eggs in ginger syrup

FAMILY MENU FOR 6 PEOPLE

Golden baskets

Mixed vegetables with sweet and sour sauce

Garlic shrimp

Red curry chicken with Thai baby eggplants

Bean sprouts and tofu soup

Boiled jasmine rice

Black sticky rice with egg custard (make
double quantities)

FAMILY MENU FOR 6 PEOPLE

Chicken satay served with peanut sauce and
cucumber relish

Stir-fried mixed vegetables

Spicy minced duck

Massaman beef curry

Hot and sour soup with seafood

Boiled jasmine rice

Watermelon sorbet

FAMILY SEAFOOD MENU FOR 6 PEOPLE

Grilled squid salad with cashews

Fish with ginger sauce

Seafood curry steamed in banana leaves

Jungle curry with mixed vegetables

Garlic shrimp

Boiled jasmine rice

Lemongrass and lime sorbet

BUFFET MENU FOR 20 PEOPLE

Vegetable curry in filo parcels

Thai dim sum served with chili and lime
sauce

Green papaya salad with chili and lime

Spicy sliced steak

Hot and sour vermicelli with shrimp

Pan-fried fishcakes with green beans served
with cucumber relish

Fried rice with shrimp, crab, and curry
powder

Fresh egg noodles with mixed vegetables

Fresh fruit platter

BANQUET MENU FOR 8–10 PEOPLE

Golden baskets

Spring rolls served with garlic and chili sauce
or sesame oil

Chicken satay served with peanut sauce and
cucumber relish

Red curry with duck and lychees

Stir-fried mixed vegetables

Grilled fish with three-flavor sauce

Hot and sour soup with seafood

Chicken with cashews

Thai-fried noodles with shrimp

Boiled jasmine rice

Sticky rice with mango (make double
quantities)

Basic recipes

At the heart of Thai cooking are the curry pastes, sauces, stocks, relishes, and rice, a selection of which are included here. Stock will keep well in the refrigerator for 2–3 days or for 2 months in sealed food containers in the freezer.

Beef stock

INGREDIENTS *7½ cups cold water* ‖ *13 oz beef or veal bones with some meat on, roughly chopped* ‖ *1 carrot, roughly chopped* ‖ *1 celery stick, roughly chopped* ‖ *1 onion, quartered* ‖ *1 inch fresh ginger root, peeled and sliced* ‖ *2 cilantro plants, including roots* ‖ *5 black peppercorns, crushed*

ONE Put all the ingredients in a large saucepan and bring to a boil. Reduce heat and simmer for 1½ hours. From time to time, skim off any fat that rises to the surface. **TWO** Strain the stock into a clean bowl, discard the solids and other unwanted parts, and let cool. **THREE** Put the stock in the refrigerator for 4–5 hours or overnight. Remove any fat that has solidified on the surface and use as needed.

Makes about 4 cups

Chicken stock

INGREDIENTS *7½ cups water* ‖ *8 oz chicken drumsticks, wings, and giblets, well rinsed* ‖ *1 carrot, peeled and roughly chopped* ‖ *1 celery stick, roughly chopped* ‖ *1 onion, quartered* ‖ *1 inch fresh ginger root, peeled and sliced* ‖ *2 cilantro plants, including roots* ‖ *5 peppercorns, crushed*

ONE Put all the ingredients in a large saucepan and bring to a boil. Reduce heat to between medium and low and simmer for 1½ hours. From time to time, skim off any fat that rises to the surface. **TWO** Transfer the stock into a clean bowl and let cool. **THREE** Remove the chicken pieces and reserve them for later use and discard the other solids. **FOUR** Put the stock in the refrigerator for 4–5 hours or overnight. Remove any fat that has solidified on the surface and use as needed.

Makes about 4 cups

Vegetable stock

INGREDIENTS *5 cups cold water* ‖ *1 carrot, roughly chopped* ‖ *1 celery stick, roughly chopped* ‖ *1 onion, quartered* ‖ *4 oz Chinese white lettuce* ‖ *½ inch fresh ginger root, peeled and sliced* ‖ *2 whole cilantro plants, including roots* ‖ *5 peppercorns, crushed*

ONE Put all the ingredients in a large saucepan and bring to a boil over high heat. When the water starts to boil, reduce heat to between medium and low and simmer for 30 minutes. Skim from time to time as necessary. **TWO** Strain the stock into a clean bowl and use as needed.

Makes about 4 cups

Seafood stock

INGREDIENTS *5 cups cold water* ‖ *1 carrot, peeled and roughly chopped* ‖ *1 celery stick, roughly chopped* ‖ *1 onion, quartered* ‖ *2 cilantro plants, including roots* ‖ *7 oz fish heads, tails, and bones or shrimp heads, shells, and tails* ‖ *5 black peppercorns, crushed*

ONE Put the water, carrot, celery, onion, and cilantro in a large saucepan and heat for 10 minutes or until boiling. **TWO** Add the fish heads, tails, and bones or shrimp heads, shells, and tails and the peppercorns and continue simmering over medium to low heat for another 10–15 minutes, skimming from time to time. **THREE** Strain the stock into a clean bowl, discard the solids and unwanted parts, and let cool. **FOUR** Put the stock in the refrigerator and use as needed.

Makes about 7½ cups

Massaman curry paste

INGREDIENTS *2 dried, long red chilies, each about 5 inches long, or 4 dried, small red chilies, each about 2 inches long* ‖ *1 lemongrass stalk (white part only), about 5 inches long, finely sliced* ‖ *1 inch fresh galangal, peeled and finely sliced* ‖ *5 kaffir lime leaves, finely chopped* ‖ *4 garlic cloves, roughly chopped* ‖ *3 shallots, roughly chopped* ‖ *4 cilantro roots, finely chopped* ‖ *1 teaspoon shrimp paste* ‖ *1 teaspoon ground allspice* ‖ *1 tablespoon paprika* ‖ *¼ teaspoon ground white pepper*

ONE Remove the stems and slit the chilies lengthwise with a sharp knife. Discard all the seeds and roughly chop the flesh. Soak the chilies in hot water for 2 minutes or until soft, then drain. **TWO** Use a mortar and pestle or blender to grind the chilies, lemongrass, galangal, and kaffir lime leaves into a paste. **THREE** Add the garlic, shallots, and cilantro roots and pound together. **FOUR** Add the remaining ingredients and pound until the mixture becomes a smooth paste.

Makes about 1 cup

Yellow curry paste

INGREDIENTS *2–3 dried, long red chilies, each about 5 inches long, or 5 dried, small red chilies, each about 2 inches long* ‖ *2 lemongrass stalks (white part only), each about 5 inches long, finely sliced* ‖ *2 garlic cloves, roughly chopped* ‖ *3 shallots, roughly chopped* ‖ *1 tablespoon yellow curry powder* ‖ *1 teaspoon ground coriander* ‖ *1 teaspoon ground cumin*

ONE Remove the stems and slit the chilies lengthwise with a sharp knife. Discard all the seeds and roughly chop the flesh. Soak the chilies in hot water for 2 minutes or until soft, then drain. **TWO** Use a mortar and pestle or blender to grind the chilies and lemongrass into a smooth paste. **THREE** Add the garlic and shallots and then the remaining ingredients. Pound together until the mixture becomes a smooth paste.

Makes about 1 cup

Green curry paste

INGREDIENTS *4–5 small green chilies, each about 2 inches long ‖ 1 lemongrass stalk (white part only), about 5 inches long, finely sliced ‖ 1 inch fresh galangal, peeled and finely sliced ‖ 5 kaffir lime leaves, finely chopped ‖ 4 garlic cloves, roughly chopped ‖ 3 shallots, roughly chopped ‖ 5 cilantro roots, finely chopped ‖ small handful Thai sweet basil leaves, roughly chopped ‖ small handful cilantro leaves, roughly chopped ‖ 1 teaspoon shrimp paste ‖ 1 teaspoon ground coriander ‖ 1 teaspoon ground cumin ‖ ¼ teaspoon ground white pepper*

ONE Remove the stems from the chilies. Use a mortar and pestle or blender to grind the chilies, lemongrass, galangal, and kaffir lime leaves into a paste. **TWO** Add the garlic, shallots, cilantro roots, basil, and cilantro leaves and grind them together. **THREE** Add the remaining ingredients and grind together until the mixture becomes a smooth paste.

Makes about ½ cup

Red curry paste

INGREDIENTS *3–4 dried, long red chilies, each about 5 inches long, or 8 dried, small red chilies, each about 2 inches long ‖ · 1 lemongrass stalk (white part only), about 5 inches long, finely sliced ‖ 1 inch fresh galangal, peeled and finely sliced ‖ 5 kaffir lime leaves, finely chopped ‖ 4 garlic cloves, roughly chopped ‖ 3 shallots, roughly chopped ‖ 5 cilantro roots, finely chopped ‖ 2 teaspoons shrimp paste ‖ 1 teaspoon ground coriander ‖ 1 tablespoon paprika*

ONE Remove the stems and slit the chilies lengthwise with a sharp knife. Discard all the seeds and roughly chop the flesh. Soak the chilies in hot water for 2 minutes or until soft, then drain. **TWO** Use a mortar and pestle or blender to grind the chilies, lemongrass, galangal, and kaffir lime leaves into a paste. **THREE** Add the garlic, shallots, and cilantro roots and grind together. **FOUR** Add the remaining ingredients and grind until the mixture forms a smooth paste.

Makes about ½ cup

Dry curry paste

INGREDIENTS *2 dried, long red chilies, each about 5 inches long, or 3 dried, small red chilies, each about 2 inches long ‖ 1 lemongrass stalk (white part only), about 5 inches long, finely sliced ‖ 1 inch fresh galangal, peeled and finely sliced ‖ 5 kaffir lime leaves, finely chopped ‖ 4 garlic cloves, roughly chopped ‖ 3 shallots, roughly chopped ‖ 5 cilantro roots, finely chopped ‖ 1 teaspoon shrimp paste ‖ 1 tablespoon paprika ‖ 1 teaspoon ground cumin*

ONE Remove the stems and slit the chilies lengthwise with a sharp knife. Discard all the seeds and roughly chop the flesh. Soak the chilies in hot water for 2 minutes or until soft, then drain. **TWO** Use a mortar and pestle or blender to grind the chilies, lemongrass, galangal, and kaffir lime leaves into a paste. **THREE** Add the garlic, shallots, and cilantro roots and grind until smooth. **FOUR** Add the remaining ingredients and grind together until the mixture forms a smooth paste.

Makes about ⅓ cup

Peanut sauce

INGREDIENTS *1 cup peanuts ‖ 1 tablespoon sunflower oil ‖ ¾ cup canned unsweetened coconut milk, shaken well ‖ ¾ cup Vegetable Stock (see page 16) or water ‖ 2 tablespoons Tamarind Purée (see page 22) or lemon juice ‖ 2 tablespoons palm or coconut sugar ‖ 1 tablespoon fish sauce ‖ 2 tablespoons dried bread crumbs*

CHILI PASTE *2 dried, long red chilies, each about 5 inches long ‖ 1 lemongrass stalk (white part only), about 4 inches long, finely sliced ‖ 3 garlic cloves, roughly chopped ‖ 2 shallots, roughly chopped ‖ 3 cilantro roots, finely chopped ‖ 3 kaffir lime leaves, finely chopped*

ONE Dry-fry the peanuts for 8–10 minutes, shaking the pan frequently. When cool, roughly chop. **TWO** Make the paste. Prepare the chilies as for the curry pastes (see above). **THREE** Use a mortar and pestle or blender to grind the chilies, lemongrass, and garlic. Add the shallots, cilantro roots, and kaffir lime leaves and grind to a smooth paste. **FOUR** Heat the oil in a nonstick saucepan and stir-fry the chili paste over medium heat for 1–2 minutes. **FIVE** Add the coconut milk, stock, tamarind purée or lemon juice, sugar, and fish sauce and simmer for 4–5 minutes. **SIX** Add the bread crumbs and peanuts, stir thoroughly, and serve with Chicken Satay *(see page 30)*.

Makes sufficient quantity for Chicken Satay

Garlic and chili sauce

INGREDIENTS *3 small red and green chilies, lightly crushed* ‖ *4 garlic cloves, finely chopped* ‖ *2 tablespoons lemon juice* ‖ *1 tablespoon light soy sauce*

ONE Mix all the ingredients in a small bowl. **TWO** Set aside and serve instead of Ginger and Chili Sauce with Spring Rolls *(see page 37)*.

Makes ⅓ cup

Cucumber relish

INGREDIENTS *⅔ cup white rice vinegar* ‖ *2 teaspoons sugar* ‖ *¼ teaspoon salt* ‖ *4 inches cucumber, peeled, quartered, and finely sliced* ‖ *1 small carrot, peeled, quartered, and finely sliced* ‖ *1 shallot, finely sliced* ‖ *1 long red chili, stemmed, seeded, and finely sliced*

ONE In a small saucepan, boil the vinegar, sugar, and salt until the sugar has dissolved. Let cool. **TWO** Pour the liquid over the cucumber, carrot, shallot, and chilies. Let stand for 30 minutes before serving with Chicken Satay *(see page 30)* or Pan-Fried Fishcakes *(see page 34)*.

Makes sufficient quantity for Chicken Satay and Pan-Fried Fishcakes

Hot chili flake sauce

INGREDIENTS *2 tablespoons lime or lemon juice* ‖ *1 tablespoon light soy sauce* ‖ *1½ teaspoons crushed red pepper flakes or ground red pepper*

ONE Mix together all the ingredients in a small bowl. **TWO** Serve with dishes such as Steamed Crabs *(see page 29)*.

Makes ⅓ cup

Sesame oil sauce

INGREDIENTS *1 teaspoon sesame seeds* ‖ *½ teaspoon sesame oil* ‖ *1 tablespoon Vegetable Stock (see page 16)* ‖ *or water* ‖ *1 tablespoon light soy sauce*

ONE Dry-fry the sesame seeds in a small pan for 1–2 minutes or until lightly browned. Let cool for 5 minutes. **TWO** Use a spoon to mash and break some of the sesame seeds to release their flavor. **THREE** Mix seeds with remaining ingredients and serve.

Makes about ¼ cup

Ginger and chili sauce

INGREDIENTS *2 oz fresh ginger root, peeled* ‖ *1 tablespoon Vegetable Stock (see page 16) or water* ‖ *1 tablespoon light soy sauce* ‖ *½ long red chili, stemmed, seeded, and finely chopped*

ONE Grate ginger and squeeze well to yield 1 tablespoon juice. **TWO** Mix juice with remaining ingredients and serve.

Makes about ¼ cup

Chili and lime sauce

INGREDIENTS *1 long red chili or 3–4 small chilies* ‖ *2 garlic cloves, finely chopped* ‖ *3 tablespoons lime or lemon juice* ‖ *1 teaspoon fish sauce*

ONE Remove the stems and slit the chili(es) lengthwise with a sharp knife. Finely slice the flesh. **TWO** Mix all the ingredients in a small bowl. **THREE** Serve with dishes such as Thai Dim Sum *(see page 33)*.

Makes ½ cup

Tamarind purée

INGREDIENTS *2 oz dried tamarind pulp* ‖ *⅔ cup boiling water*

ONE Put the tamarind pulp in a bowl and soak it with the boiling water for 8–10 minutes. **TWO** Mash the pulp with a spoon or fork to help it dissolve. Strain the thick liquid into a small, clean bowl and discard the fibers and seeds.

Makes 6–7 tablespoons

Boiled jasmine rice

INGREDIENTS *2½ cups jasmine rice* ‖ *2 cups room-temperature water (use more if necessary)*

ONE Place the jasmine rice in a bowl with clean water. Scoop the rice through with your fingers 4–5 times and drain. Transfer rice to a saucepan and add the measured water. **TWO** Cook over high heat, stirring frequently, until boiling. Turn down the heat as low as possible and cover, leaving a small gap between the lid and the side of the pan. **THREE** Simmer gently for 10–15 minutes or until the water has been absorbed. **FOUR** Remove from heat and let stand for another 10 minutes. Remove the lid and stir the rice gently with a rice paddle to fluff and separate the grains. Serve immediately.

Serves 4

Boiled Thai brown rice

INGREDIENTS *2½ cups Thai brown rice* ‖ *3¾ cups room-temperature water (use more if necessary)*

ONE Place the brown rice in a bowl with clean water. Scoop the rice through with your fingers 4–5 times and drain. Transfer rice to a saucepan and add the measured water. **TWO** Cook over high heat, stirring frequently, until boiling. Turn down the heat as low as possible and cover, leaving a small gap between the lid and the side of the pan. **THREE** Simmer gently for 25–30 minutes or until the water has been absorbed. (Check that no water remains at the bottom of the saucepan.) **FOUR** Remove from heat and let stand for another 10 minutes. Remove the lid and stir the rice gently with a rice paddle to separate the grains. Serve immediately.

Serves 4

Steamed sticky rice

INGREDIENTS *2½ cups sticky rice*

ONE Soak rice in a bowl of water for at least 3 hours. **TWO** Drain and transfer to a bamboo basket lined with a double thickness of cheesecloth. Spread the rice in the steamer. **THREE** Bring the water in a pan or wok to a rolling boil and, taking care not to burn your hand, set the bamboo basket over the water. Reduce heat, cover, and steam for 20–25 minutes or until rice swells and is glistening and tender. Check and replenish the water as necessary every 10 minutes or so. **FOUR** When rice is cooked, transfer to a tray or large plate and spread out to cool quickly so that it does not become soggy.

Serves 4

Soups and appetizers

Golden baskets

Golden baskets are a wonderful appetizer. They are attractive to look at and simple to make. You can find frozen spring roll sheets in Asian supermarkets, and the other basic ingredients are widely available. The baskets can be made the day before they are needed and stored in an airtight container. Spoon the filling into the baskets 30 minutes before serving.

INGREDIENTS *7 oz package spring roll sheets, 5 x 5 inches, or filo pastry, thawed if frozen*

FILLING *1–1½ tablespoons sunflower oil* ‖ *2 garlic cloves, finely chopped* ‖ *7 oz ground chicken or shrimp* ‖ *¼ cup carrots, finely diced* ‖ *¼ cup corn kernels, thawed if frozen* ‖ *¼ cup green peas, thawed if frozen* ‖ *½ cup red bell pepper, seeded and finely diced* ‖ *1 tablespoon light soy sauce* ‖ *½ teaspoon ground white pepper* ‖ *pinch curry powder* ‖ *1 green onion, finely chopped*

TO SERVE *30 cilantro leaves* ‖ *2 long red chilies, stemmed, seeded, and finely sliced*

ONE Make the filling. Heat oil in a nonstick wok or skillet and stir-fry garlic over medium heat until lightly browned. Add the chicken or shrimp, crumbling and breaking up the meat until it has separated and cooked. **TWO** Add the carrots, corn, peas, and red bell pepper and stir-fry for 1–2 minutes. Add the soy sauce, ground white pepper, curry powder, and green onion, combine well, and set aside. **THREE** Cut the spring roll sheets or filo pastry into 60 squares, each 2½ x 2½ inches. Lay 2 squares in each indentation in a muffin pan used for making 1½ inch muffins, overlapping the squares so that the top sheet is at an angle of 45 degrees to the bottom one. Prepare 30 baskets and bake in a preheated oven, 350°F, for 10–12 minutes or until crispy and golden brown. Carefully remove baskets and let cool slightly. **FOUR** Spoon the filling into the baskets and serve at room temperature, garnished with a cilantro leaf and some chili slices.

Makes 30 baskets; serves 4–6 as a starter

NUTRIENT ANALYSIS PER BASKET 153 kJ – 37 cal – 2 g protein – 5 g carbohydrate – 0 g sugars – 1 g fat – 0 g saturated fat – 0 g fiber – 40 mg sodium

HEALTHY TIP You can use a variety of vegetables in these baskets, which will help provide you with a range of phytonutrients.

Vegetable curry in filo parcels
I use filo pastry for these curry triangles and bake them in the oven rather than deep-frying them as I would curry puffs.

INGREDIENTS *1 tablespoon sunflower oil* ‖ *2–3 garlic cloves, finely chopped* ‖ *½ oz cilantro roots (about 2 roots), finely chopped* ‖ *½ inch fresh ginger root, peeled and finely chopped* ‖ *1 onion, finely chopped* ‖ *½ cup carrots, finely diced* ‖ *½ cup red bell pepper, seeded and finely diced* ‖ *½ cup corn kernels, thawed if frozen* ‖ *½ cup green peas, thawed if frozen* ‖ *1 lb potatoes, boiled in their skins and cut into small dice* ‖ *1½ tablespoons light soy sauce* ‖ *1 teaspoon curry powder* ‖ *pinch ground white pepper* ‖ *¼ long red chili, stemmed, seeded, and finely sliced (optional)* ‖ *2 x 9 oz packages filo sheets, thawed if frozen* ‖ *2–3 tablespoons sunflower oil, for brushing*

ONE Heat oil in a nonstick wok or skillet and stir-fry garlic over medium heat until lightly browned. Add cilantro roots, ginger, and onion and cook over medium heat for 1–2 minutes. **TWO** Add the carrots, red bell pepper, corn, and peas and stir-fry for another 2–3 minutes. **THREE** Stir in the potatoes, soy sauce, curry powder, ground white pepper, and chili (if using). Let cool to room temperature. **FOUR** Meanwhile, cut 20 filo pastry strips, each 5 x 10 inches. Place 3 filo strips with the short sides in front of you and keep the remaining sheets in a plastic bag to prevent them from drying out. **FIVE** Put 2 tablespoons of the filling on the bottom left-hand corner of the pastry. Fold up the corner to make a triangle and continue to flip the triangle along the length of the filo strip to wrap the filling in the pastry. **SIX** Place the filo triangle on a lightly oiled baking sheet. Repeat with the remaining filling and filo rectangles, placing them on the baking sheet so that there is a slight gap between each one. Brush each triangle with a little oil. **SEVEN** Bake the parcels in a preheated oven, 350°F, for 5 minutes. Turn them over and bake for another 2–3 minutes or until crispy and golden brown. Serve warm or at room temperature.

Makes 20; serves 6–8 as a starter

NUTRIENT ANALYSIS PER SERVING 1858 kJ – 444 cal – 12 g protein – 76 g carbohydrate – 4 g sugars – 11 g fat – 1 g saturated fat – 3 g fiber – 470 mg sodium

HEALTHY TIP Unlike most other types of pastry, filo contains little fat. In 3½ oz filo pastry there are just 2 g of fat and 300 cal. The same weight of pastry crust contains 29 g fat and 449 cal.

Steamed crabs

A seaside favorite, steamed crabs make a lovely starter to a Thai meal. Serve with Hot Chili Flake Sauce *(see page 20)* or Ginger and Chili Sauce *(see page 21)*.

INGREDIENTS *4 lb fresh, uncooked crabs (3–4 crabs)*

ONE Prepare the crabs *(see page 12)*. **TWO** Fill a wok or steamer pan with water. Insert the bamboo steamer basket or steamer rack, cover the wok, and bring the water to a boil over high heat. **THREE** Place the crabs on a baking dish that will fit on the rack of the bamboo steamer basket but that is slightly larger than the crabs. **FOUR** Taking care not to burn your hand, set the dish inside the steamer basket and simmer for 20–25 minutes or until crabs are cooked. Check and replenish the water every 10 minutes or so. **FIVE** Remove crabs from the steamer and serve them hot or warm.

Serves 4 as a starter

NUTRIENT ANALYSIS PER SERVING 547 kJ – 130 cal – 20 g protein – 1 g carbohydrate – 0 g sugars – 5 g fat – 1 g saturated fat – 0 g fiber – 370 mg sodium

HEALTHY TIP Crab is an excellent source of protein and is low in fat and calories. It also supplies zinc, copper, calcium, magnesium, and iron.

Chicken satay

Satay consists of skewers of meat—chicken as in this recipe, or beef, lamb, turkey, or a combination of these—marinated in coconut milk and spices and grilled quickly over charcoal. Originating in Indonesia, this tasty dish has traveled north up the peninsula, becoming adapted to suit local taste. You will need 40 bamboo skewers, each 7–8 inches long. Soak them in water for about an hour before you use them so that they do not burn during cooking. Serve hot with Peanut Sauce *(see page 19)* and Cucumber Relish *(see page 20)*.

INGREDIENTS *2 lb boneless, skinless chicken breasts*

MARINADE *2 shallots, roughly chopped* ‖ *3 garlic cloves, roughly chopped* ‖ *4 cilantro roots, finely chopped* ‖ *1 inch fresh ginger root, peeled and sliced* ‖ *1 tablespoon ground coriander* ‖ *1 tablespoon ground cumin* ‖ *1 tablespoon ground turmeric* ‖ *1 teaspoon curry powder* ‖ *1½ tablespoons light soy sauce* ‖ *2 tablespoons sunflower oil* ‖ *¾ cup canned unsweetened coconut milk, well stirred* ‖ *⅔ cup Chicken Stock (see page 15) or water* ‖ *1 tablespoon palm or coconut sugar (see note page 11)*

ONE Cut chicken into strips 1½ x 4 inches long and ¼ inch thick and place in a mixing bowl. **TWO** Make the marinade. Use a mortar and pestle or food processor to blend the shallots, garlic, cilantro roots, and ginger into a paste. Add the mixture and the remaining marinade ingredients to the chicken. Mix thoroughly with a spoon or your fingers. Cover with plastic wrap and refrigerate for at least 5 hours or overnight, turning the chicken occasionally. **THREE** Thread a piece of the marinated chicken onto each presoaked bamboo skewer as if you were sewing a piece of material. (If the pieces are small, use 2 on each stick.) **FOUR** Preheat the grill or broiler to high heat and cook the satay sticks for 5–7 minutes on each side or until they are cooked through and slightly charred. Turn frequently and brush the marinade sauce over the meat during cooking.

Makes 40 sticks; serves 6–8 as a starter

NUTRIENT ANALYSIS PER SERVING 1306 kJ – 312 cal – 38 g protein – 7 g carbohydrate – 5 g sugars – 5 g fat – 6 g saturated fat– 0 g fiber – 160 mg sodium

HEALTHY TIP The white meat of a chicken is lower in calories, lower in fat, and higher in protein than dark meat. Use free-range or organic chicken for the best flavor.

Savory egg custard

Egg custard does not have to be a dessert. This savory version is a terrific addition to a meal where several other main dishes, such as curries and stir-fries, are being served.

INGREDIENTS *4 large eggs* ‖ *⅔ cup Vegetable Stock (see page 16)* ‖ *1 tablespoon light soy sauce* ‖ *2 green onions, finely chopped* ‖ *½ inch fresh ginger root, peeled and finely sliced*

TO SERVE *cilantro leaves* ‖ *ground white pepper*

ONE Fill a wok or steamer pan with water. Insert the bamboo steamer basket or steamer rack, cover, and bring to a boil over medium heat. **TWO** Meanwhile, in a heatproof bowl, beat the eggs with the stock, soy sauce, green onions, and ginger. **THREE** Taking care not to burn your hand, set the custard bowl inside the steamer basket and simmer for 13–15 minutes or until the egg custard has set. Season with ground white pepper. Serve hot or warm with a few cilantro leaves.

Serves 4 with 3 other main dishes

NUTRIENT ANALYSIS PER SERVING 360 kJ – 87 cal – 7 g protein – 1 g carbohydrate – 0 g sugars – 6 g fat – 2 g saturated fat – 0 g fiber – 78 mg sodium

HEALTHY TIP In a single egg you get 5.5 g of protein, more than 10 percent of the daily requirement, at a cost of just 68 calories.

Thai dim sum

Originating in China, dim sum has long been enjoyed in Thailand where it is often eaten as a substantial snack. It also makes an excellent starter to a larger meal. Serve with Chili and Lime Sauce *(see page 21)*.

INGREDIENTS *about 30 yellow wonton sheets or wrappers, each 3 x 3 inches* ‖ *sunflower oil, for brushing*

FILLING *10 oz ground shrimp* ‖ *4 oz canned crab meat, drained* ‖ *3 oz canned water chestnuts, drained and roughly chopped* ‖ *2 garlic cloves, finely chopped* ‖ *2 green onions (white part only), finely sliced* ‖ *1 tablespoon oyster sauce* ‖ *1 tablespoon soy sauce* ‖ *1 teaspoon sesame oil* ‖ *⅛ teaspoon ground white pepper*

TO SERVE *30 cilantro leaves* ‖ *¼ long red chili, stemmed, seeded, and finely sliced*

ONE Make the filling. Mix all ingredients together in a mixing bowl. **TWO** Spoon about 1 tablespoon of the mixture into the middle of each wonton sheet. Pull up the sheet to form a bag but leave an opening about ½ inch wide at the top so that the filling is not entirely covered. **THREE** Fill a wok or a steamer pan with water, place the bamboo steamer basket or steamer rack over the water, cover, and place over high heat. Brush a plate with a little sunflower oil and place the dim sum on it, making sure they are packed closely together. Set the plate inside the steamer basket carefully and simmer for 10 minutes over medium heat. (You will probably need to steam the dim sum in two or three batches.) **FOUR** To serve, garnish the top of each dim sum with a cilantro leaf and some chili slices.

Makes 30; serves 4–6 as a starter

NUTRIENT ANALYSIS PER SERVING 1380 kJ – 330 cal – 22 g protein – 36 g carbohydrate – 1 g sugars – 11 g fat – 1 g saturated fat – 0 g fiber – 970 mg sodium

HEALTHY TIP Water chestnuts provide small amounts of potassium and iron, but their main advantage is that they contain no fat and few calories.

Pan-fried fishcakes with green beans

Thai fishcakes are especially popular outside Thailand, but they are not always made with the right blend of flavors. Here is an authentic Thai recipe for you to enjoy. If you do not have time to make the chili paste, use 1 tablespoon of store-bought red curry paste. Serve with Cucumber Relish *(see page 20)*.

INGREDIENTS *1 lb white fish fillet, skinned, cleaned, and roughly chopped* ‖ *1 tablespoon fish sauce* ‖ *1½ tablespoons cornstarch* ‖ *1 egg* ‖ *2 oz green beans, finely sliced* ‖ *5 kaffir lime leaves, finely sliced* ‖ *sunflower oil for frying*

CHILI PASTE *2 dried, long red chilies, each about 5 inches long* ‖ *1 lemongrass stalk (white part only), 3 inches long, finely sliced* ‖ *3 garlic cloves, roughly chopped* ‖ *2 shallots, roughly chopped* ‖ *2 cilantro roots, cleaned and finely chopped*

ONE Make the chili paste. Remove the stems and slit the chilies lengthwise with a sharp knife. Discard the seeds. Roughly chop the flesh, soak it in hot water for 2 minutes or until soft, then drain. **TWO** Use a mortar and pestle to pound the chilies, lemongrass, garlic, shallots, and cilantro roots until the mixture forms a smooth paste. **THREE** Use a food processor or a blender to mince the fish fillets. Add the chili paste (or red curry paste), fish sauce, cornstarch, and egg and blend briefly until smooth. Spoon the mixture into a bowl and mix with the green beans and kaffir lime leaves. **FOUR** Use a tablespoon or damp hands to shape the fish mixture into thin, flat cakes, 2 inches across, and put them on a baking sheet lined with waxed paper while you use all the mixture. **FIVE** Heat a little sunflower oil in a nonstick skillet and gently fry 8–10 fishcakes at a time (depending on the size of your skillet), making sure there is a slight gap between each one. Fry for 2–3 minutes on each side or until cooked and lightly browned. Add a little oil to the pan before cooking each batch.

Makes 25–30; serves 6–8 as a starter

NUTRIENT ANALYSIS PER FISHCAKE 159 kJ – 38 cal – 4 g protein – 2 g carbohydrate – 0 g sugars – 2 g fat – 0 g saturated fat – 0 g fiber – 54 mg sodium

HEALTHY TIP These pan-fried fishcakes are a much healthier alternative to the usual deep-fried version.

Dry wonton

This is a popular one-meal dish in noodle restaurants. There are two types of wonton: those that are served in soups, and those, as in this recipe, that are served in various dry dishes.

INGREDIENTS *40 wonton sheets or wrappers, 3 x 3 inches* ‖ *10 oz raw shrimp* ‖ *1½ tablespoons sunflower oil* ‖ *4–5 garlic cloves, finely chopped* ‖ *8 oz Chinese cabbage (cho sum) or spinach leaves, roughly chopped* ‖ *8 oz fresh bean sprouts, tails removed* ‖ *2 tablespoons light soy sauce* ‖ *1 tablespoon preserved radish (optional)*

FILLING *1 lb ground shrimp, pork, or chicken* ‖ *4 garlic cloves, finely chopped* ‖ *4 cilantro roots, finely chopped* ‖ *¼ teaspoon ground white pepper*

TO SERVE *4 oz cooked crab claws (about 8 claws) or cooked crab meat* ‖ *2 green onions, finely sliced diagonally* ‖ *ground white pepper*

ONE Make the filling. Combine the ground shrimp or meat with the garlic, cilantro roots, and ground white pepper. **TWO** Spoon a little of the filling mixture into the middle of each wonton sheet. Brush the edges with water and gather up the sheet, squeezing the corners together to make a little purse. **THREE** Prepare the shrimp *(see page 12)*. **FOUR** Heat the oil in a nonstick wok or skillet and stir-fry the garlic over medium heat until lightly browned. Transfer to a small bowl. **FIVE** Cook the Chinese cabbage in boiling water for 1–2 minutes. Use a sieve or coarse-meshed strainer to drain the leaves, then put them into a mixing bowl. **SIX** Cook the shrimp in boiling water for 1–2 minutes or until they open and turn pink. Remove the shrimp with a slotted spoon and put them in the mixing bowl. **SEVEN** Gently drop each wonton purse into the boiling water and cook for 2–3 minutes or until the ground shrimp inside is cooked. Drain and add to the mixing bowl. Add the sautéed garlic and oil, bean sprouts, soy sauce, and preserved radish (if using) to the mixing bowl and toss. Spoon the mixture into 8 individual serving bowls, season with ground white pepper, and serve immediately with crab claws and green onion slices.

Serves 8 as an appetizer or 4 as a main dish

NUTRIENT ANALYSIS PER SERVING 1645 kJ – 396 cal – 34 g protein – 48 g carbohydrate – 2 g sugars – 7 g fat – 1 g saturated fat – 0 g fiber – 719 mg sodium

HEALTHY TIP Bean sprouts are a good source of vitamin C and also contain small amounts of the B-group vitamins as well as potassium and iron.

Spring rolls

These savory rolls are popular throughout Southeast Asia. The Thai version is a delicate cross between Chinese and Vietnamese styles. Instead of being deep-fried, the rolls are wrapped with sheets of filo pastry and baked in the oven until they are golden and crispy. Serve with Ginger and Chili Sauce or Sesame Oil Sauce *(see page 21)*.

INGREDIENTS *4 oz vermicelli or dried wun sen noodles* ‖ *½ oz dried black fungus* ‖ *1 tablespoon sunflower oil, plus extra for brushing* ‖ *3–4 garlic cloves, finely chopped* ‖ *5 oz fresh bean sprouts* ‖ *1 small carrot, finely grated* ‖ *½ cup green peas, thawed if frozen* ‖ *½ cup corn kernels, thawed if frozen* ‖ *½ inch fresh ginger root, peeled and finely grated* ‖ *2 tablespoons light soy sauce* ‖ *¼ teaspoon ground white pepper* ‖ *3 x 9 oz packages filo pastry, thawed if frozen*

ONE Soak noodles in hot water for 1–2 minutes or until soft. Drain and cut into small pieces. Soak dried black fungus in hot water for 2–3 minutes or until soft. Drain and finely chop. **TWO** Heat oil in a nonstick wok or skillet and stir-fry garlic over medium heat until lightly browned. Add noodles, dried black fungus, bean sprouts, carrots, peas, corn, ginger, soy sauce, and ground white pepper. Cook for another 4–5 minutes and let cool. **THREE** Cut 50 filo pastry squares, each 4 x 4 inches. **FOUR** Keep the filo squares you are not using in a plastic bag to prevent them from drying out while you work. Place 2 filo squares on a work surface and spoon 2 teaspoons of the filling along the side nearest to you and about 1 inch from the edge. Bring the edge up, then roll it away from you, half a turn over the filling. Fold the sides into the center to enclose the filling, then wrap and seal the seam tightly. Repeat until you have used all the filling and filo squares. Place the spring rolls seam side down on a lightly greased baking sheet, making sure there is a slight gap between each one, and brush each one with a little oil. **FIVE** Bake in a preheated oven, 350°F, for 5 minutes. Turn over, bake for another 2–3 minutes or until crispy and golden brown. Serve warm or at room temperature.

Makes 50; serves 10–15 as a starter

NUTRIENT ANALYSIS PER SPRING ROLL 290 kJ – 69 cal – 2 g protein – 13 g carbohydrate – 0 g sugars – 1 g fat – 0 g saturated fat – 0 g fiber – 85 mg sodium

HEALTHY TIP Frozen vegetables often contain more vitamin C than fresh vegetables. Frozen peas, for example, retain 60–70 percent of their vitamin C content after freezing and maintain that level throughout storage.

Barbecued pork spare ribs with honey

We can eat outside in Thailand at any time of the year, so we have lots of barbecues. Everyone loves this tasty dish, especially children, and it can be served as a starter or as finger food at a party. If possible, ask your butcher to prepare baby back ribs for you.

INGREDIENTS *2 lb pork spare ribs, cut into 4–5 inch lengths ‖ 3 garlic cloves, finely chopped ‖ 3 cilantro roots, cleaned and finely chopped, or 1 teaspoon ground coriander ‖ 2 tablespoons honey ‖ 2 tablespoons tomato ketchup ‖ 1 tablespoon light soy sauce ‖ ½ teaspoon ground white pepper ‖ ¼ teaspoon ground allspice (optional)*

TO SERVE *1 red chili, finely sliced ‖ 1 green onion, finely sliced*

ONE In a large mixing bowl, combine all ingredients with your fingers or a spoon. Cover with plastic wrap and leave for at least 3 hours or, if time allows, overnight in the refrigerator. **TWO** Place the ribs with all the marinade in a baking dish and cook in a preheated oven, 350°F, for 45 minutes to 1 hour, basting several times during cooking. Broil for another 5 minutes on each side until well browned and slightly charred. **THREE** Alternatively, preheat a grill or broiler to medium heat. Grill the pork, turning several times and brushing frequently with the remaining sauce until the meat is cooked through and slightly charred, which should take 10–12 minutes on each side. Serve garnished with chili and green onion slices.

Serves 4 as a starter

NUTRIENT ANALYSIS PER SERVING 1215 kJ – 290 cal – 23 g protein – 14 g carbohydrate – 14 g sugars – 16 g fat – 6 g saturated fat – 0 g fiber – 320 mg sodium

HEALTHY TIP Honey is a good source of glucose and fructose and can therefore help to reduce fatigue after a strenuous workout.

Broiled shrimp and scallops with pineapple

I have used familiar ingredients in this great-tasting and attractive healthy dish. Use 7–8 inch long bamboo sticks and soak them in cold water for about an hour before you need them to prevent them from burning during cooking.

INGREDIENTS *10 oz raw shrimp* ‖ *10 oz scallops* ‖ *1 fresh pineapple, cut into 25 1 inch cubes*

MARINADE *2 garlic cloves, finely chopped* ‖ *1 tablespoon cilantro leaves, finely chopped* ‖ *1 long red chili, stemmed, seeded, and finely chopped* ‖ *1 tablespoon sesame oil* ‖ *1½ tablespoons light soy sauce* ‖ *½ teaspoon ground white pepper*

ONE Prepare the shrimp and scallops *(see page 12)*. **TWO** Put all marinade ingredients in a mixing bowl. Add the shrimp and scallops, mix together thoroughly, and marinate for at least 30 minutes. Add the pineapple chunks to the mixing bowl and mix together to coat in the marinade. **THREE** Divide the shrimp, scallops, and pineapple into separate groups. Thread the ingredients alternately onto 4 presoaked bamboo sticks. **FOUR** Broil them under high heat on the top rack of the oven for 8–10 minutes on each side.

Serves 4 as a starter

NUTRIENT ANALYSIS PER SERVING 802 kJ – 189 cal – 25 g protein – 13 g carbohydrate – 10 g sugars – 5 g fat – 1 g saturated fat – 1 g fiber – 600 mg sodium

HEALTHY TIP Scallops are a good source of vitamin B12, an important nutrient for cardiovascular health. 4 oz scallops contains one-third of the daily requirement of vitamin B12.

Bean sprout and tofu soup

Easy to make, this can be served as either a main dish or a starter. You can use ground shrimp instead of chicken or pork, if you prefer. If you cannot find cilantro roots, use 1 tablespoon finely chopped cilantro leaves instead. Big head bean sprouts, which are available in Asian supermarkets, have much larger heads than the usual type.

INGREDIENTS *10 dried black fungus* ‖ *5 oz ground chicken or pork* ‖ *3 garlic cloves, finely chopped* ‖ *2–3 cilantro roots, finely chopped* ‖ *5 oz big head bean sprouts* ‖ *12 oz soft or firm tofu* ‖ *7½ cups Chicken Stock (see page 15) or Vegetable Stock (see page 16)* ‖ *2 tablespoons light soy sauce*

TO SERVE *ground white pepper* ‖ *2 green onions, finely sliced*

ONE Soak the dried black fungus in hot water for 2–3 minutes or until soft. Drain and finely chop. **TWO** In a mixing bowl, combine the ground meat, garlic, cilantro roots, and dried black fungus. **THREE** Clean the bean sprouts and discard the tails. Drain the tofu and cut into 1 inch cubes. **FOUR** Heat the stock in a saucepan until boiling. Add the soy sauce. Use a spoon or wet fingers to shape the ground meat mixture into small balls about ½ inch across, and gently drop them into the stock. Cook for 2–3 minutes over medium heat. **FIVE** Add the tofu and bean sprouts and simmer for another 2–3 minutes, taking care not to let the tofu cubes lose their shape. Spoon into a serving bowl, season with ground white pepper, and serve garnished with green onion slices.

Serves 4 with 2 other main dishes

NUTRIENT ANALYSIS PER SERVING 630 kJ – 150 cal – 18 g protein – 8 g carbohydrate – 0 g sugars – 5 g fat – 1 g saturated fat – 0 g fiber – 36 mg sodium

HEALTHY TIP Full of nutrients yet low in calories, bean sprouts are a good source of vitamin C, and they also contain small amounts of the B group vitamins, together with potassium and iron.

Hot and sour soup with seafood

This is one of the most popular soups in Thai cuisine. If you prefer, you can include chicken, beef, or lamb instead of the seafood.

INGREDIENTS *1¼ lb mixed seafood, such as raw shrimp, squid, white fish fillet (cod or sea bass), scallops, and mussels* ‖ *3¾ cups Seafood Stock (see page 16)* ‖ *3 lemongrass stalks (white part only), each 5 inches long and cut into a tassel or bruised* ‖ *5 cilantro roots, cleaned and bruised* ‖ *2 tablespoons fish sauce* ‖ *4 oz straw or mixed mushrooms* ‖ *1 onion, quartered* ‖ *4–5 small red and green chilies, slightly crushed* ‖ *12 cherry tomatoes* ‖ *5 kaffir lime leaves, torn* ‖ *3 tablespoons lime or lemon juice* ‖ *kaffir lime leaves, finely sliced, to garnish*

ONE Prepare the mixed seafood *(see page 12)*. **TWO** Put stock, lemongrass, cilantro roots, and fish sauce in a saucepan and heat just to boiling. **THREE** Reduce heat, add seafood and cook for 2 minutes. **FOUR** Quarter any large mushrooms and add the mushrooms, onion, chilies, tomatoes, kaffir lime leaves, and lime or lemon juice. Cook for another 2–3 minutes, taking care not to let the tomatoes lose their shape. **FIVE** Pour into a serving bowl, garnish with a few sliced kaffir lime leaves, and serve.

Serves 4 with 2 other main dishes

NUTRIENT ANALYSIS PER SERVING 660 kJ – 156 cal – 26 g protein – 8 g carbohydrate – 4 g sugars – 2 g fat – 0 g saturated fat – 2 g fiber – 830 mg sodium

HEALTHY TIP Seafood contains oils composed of long chains of molecules called omega-3 fatty acids. These not only boost the immune system but also help to protect the heart against arrhythmias, a common trigger of heart attacks.

Sour ground pork soup with snake beans

In Thailand this slightly hot and sour soup is a popular addition to a main meal. Snake beans are narrow, round, stringless beans, 12–36 inches long, and can be found in Thai or Asian supermarkets. Green beans can be used as an alternative if you have trouble finding snake beans. You can also use fish or mixed seafood, which does not need to be ground, instead of meat.

INGREDIENTS *4 dried, long red chilies, each about 5 inches long, or 4 dried, small red chilies, each about 2 inches long* ‖ *7 shallots, roughly chopped* ‖ *4 garlic cloves, roughly chopped* ‖ *1 teaspoon shrimp paste* ‖ *5 cups Vegetable Stock (see page 16)* ‖ *12 oz ground pork or chicken* ‖ *12 oz snake beans, cut into 1 inch pieces* ‖ *2 tablespoons fish sauce* ‖ *5 tablespoons lemon juice*

ONE Remove the stems and slit the chilies lengthwise with a sharp knife. Discard all the seeds and roughly chop the flesh. Soak the chilies in hot water for 2 minutes or until soft, then drain. **TWO** Use a mortar and pestle to grind the chilies, shallots, garlic, and shrimp paste together until the mixture forms a smooth paste. **THREE** Put the stock in a saucepan and heat until boiling. Stir in the chili paste mixture and reduce heat to medium. **FOUR** Use a spoon or your wet hand to shape the ground meat into small balls, each about ½ inch across, and lower the balls into the stock with the beans, fish sauce, and lemon juice. Cook for 4–5 minutes and spoon into a serving bowl.

Serves 4 with 2 other main dishes

NUTRIENT ANALYSIS PER SERVING 809 kJ – 194 cal – 23 g protein – 8 g carbohydrate – 5 g sugars – 8 g fat – 2 g saturated fat – 4 g fiber – 90 mg sodium

HEALTHY TIP Fiber adds bulk or roughage to your diet. Snake beans are rich in fiber, but they should not be overcooked.

Stuffed cucumber soup with shrimp

Cucumber is wonderfully refreshing in a hot climate, and it makes a classic soup that looks as good as it tastes.

INGREDIENTS *8 pieces dried black fungus* ‖ *7 oz ground shrimp* ‖ *3 garlic cloves, finely chopped* ‖ *3 cilantro roots, finely chopped* ‖ *1 tablespoon cornstarch* ‖ *1½ lb cucumber* ‖ *3¾ cups Vegetable or Seafood Stock (see page 16)* ‖ *1½ tablespoons light soy sauce* ‖ *1 tablespoon preserved radish (optional)* ‖ *2 green onions, finely sliced*

TO SERVE *ground white pepper* ‖ *cilantro leaves*

ONE Soak the dried black fungus in hot water for 2–3 minutes or until soft. Drain and finely chop. **TWO** In a mixing bowl, combine the ground shrimp, garlic, cilantro roots, cornstarch, and dried black fungus. **THREE** Peel the cucumber and cut into 1 inch rings, discarding the seeds. Spoon the shrimp mixture into the cucumber rings. **FOUR** Put the stock in a saucepan and bring just to a boil. Add the soy sauce and preserved radish (if using). **FIVE** Gently drop the stuffed cucumber into the stock and cook over medium heat for 8–10 minutes. Add the green onions, spoon into a serving bowl, season with ground white pepper, and serve garnished with a few cilantro leaves.

Serves 4 with 2 other main dishes

NUTRIENT ANALYSIS PER SERVING 480 kJ – 115 cal – 14 g protein – 12 g carbohydrate – 3 g sugars – 1 g fat – 0 g saturated fat – 1 g fiber – 800 mg sodium

HEALTHY TIP Although most of the flesh of a cucumber is composed of water, it also contains vitamin C and caffeic acid, both of which are good for the skin.

Chicken, coconut, and galangal soup

Here is a classic Thai dish that is enjoyed by adults and children alike. The galangal and lemongrass give it plenty of flavor, but it is not too hot.

INGREDIENTS ¾ cup canned coconut milk, shaken well ‖ ¾ cup Chicken Stock *(see page 15)* ‖ 2 lemongrass stalks (white part only), each 5 inches long and cut into a tassel or bruised ‖ 2 inches fresh galangal, peeled and cut into several pieces ‖ 15 black peppercorns, crushed ‖ 13 oz boneless, skinless chicken breast fillets, sliced ‖ 1½ tablespoons fish sauce ‖ 1 tablespoon palm or coconut sugar ‖ 5 oz mixed mushrooms, such as oyster, shiitake, or button ‖ 7 oz cherry tomatoes (about 16) ‖ 2½ tablespoons lime or lemon juice ‖ 5 kaffir lime leaves, torn in half ‖ 3–5 small red and green chilies, bruised ‖ cilantro leaves, to garnish

ONE Heat the coconut milk, stock, lemongrass, galangal, and peppercorns in a saucepan or wok over medium heat and bring to a boil. **TWO** Add the chicken, fish sauce, and sugar; simmer, stirring constantly, for 5 minutes or until the chicken is cooked through. **THREE** Halve the mushrooms if they are large and remove and discard the hard stalks. Add the tomatoes and mushrooms and simmer for 2–3 minutes, making sure that the tomatoes do not lose their shape. Add the lime or lemon juice, kaffir lime leaves, and chilies for the last few seconds. Serve garnished with a few cilantro leaves.

Serves 4 with 2 other main dishes

NUTRIENT ANALYSIS PER SERVING 993 kJ – 237 cal – 24 g protein – 9 g carbohydrate – 8 g sugars – 12 g fat – 7 g saturated fat – 2 g fiber – 450 mg sodium

HEALTHY TIP Galangal aids digestion, relieves gastric distress, and alleviates the symptoms of morning sickness and motion sickness. It also has antifungal and antibacterial properties.

Salads

Green papaya salad with chili and lime

This crunchy salad is popular all over Thailand. It is mostly a tangle of pale green shreds of unripe papaya. You can also use grated carrots if it is difficult to find green papaya, but the taste is not as good. This salad goes well with sticky rice. You will be able to make one serving at a time in your mortar. To serve 4 people, multiply the ingredients by 4 and repeat the process. If you cannot find ground dried shrimp, use whole dried shrimp and grind them before preparing the salad.

INGREDIENTS *4 oz small, hard, green, unripe papaya* ‖ *2 tablespoons lime or lemon juice, plus a small piece of rind* ‖ *½ tablespoon fish sauce* ‖ *½ tablespoon palm or coconut sugar* ‖ *1–2 garlic cloves* ‖ *2 tablespoons roasted peanuts (see page 19)* ‖ *5 green beans, cut into 1 inch pieces* ‖ *½ tablespoon ground dried shrimp* ‖ *1 small red and 1 green chili* ‖ *2 oz cherry tomatoes, left whole, or 2 tomatoes, cut into 6 pieces*

ONE Use a vegetable peeler to remove the skin from the papaya. Chop the flesh into long, thin shreds or grate it. Discard any seeds and place the flesh in a bowl. **TWO** In a small bowl, mix the lime or lemon juice with the fish sauce and sugar. **THREE** Using a large mortar and pestle, pound the garlic into a paste. Add the roasted peanuts and pound them roughly with the garlic. Add the papaya and pound gently, using a spoon to scrape down the sides, turning and mixing the paste well. Add the green beans, dried shrimp, and chilies. Keep pounding and turning to bruise the ingredients. **FOUR** Add the sugar mixture, tomatoes, and a piece of lime or lemon rind. Mix and lightly pound for another minute until all the ingredients are thoroughly mixed. (As the juice comes out, pound more gently so the liquid doesn't splash.) **FIVE** Spoon the papaya salad onto a serving plate with all of the sauce remaining in the mortar and serve immediately.

Serves 1 as a starter

NUTRIENT ANALYSIS PER SERVING 1215 kJ – 290 cal – 15 g protein – 28 g carbohydrate – 13 g sugars – 13 g fat – 2 g saturated fat – 5 g fiber – 910 mg sodium

HEALTHY TIP Green papaya contains papain, an enzyme that has a soothing effect on the stomach and assists in the digestion of protein. It has a wide range of pH and will work both in an acidic stomach and an alkaline small intestine.

Cucumber salad with chicken threads

A healthy, fresh salad, this is a good addition to the menu with other dishes, especially fish curries and stir-fries. It can also be eaten on its own as a light meal.

INGREDIENTS *5 oz boneless, skinless chicken breasts* ‖ *8 oz cucumber, peeled* ‖ *2 shallots, finely sliced* ‖ *1 tablespoon roasted peanuts (see page 19), roughly chopped* ‖ *cilantro leaves, to garnish*

SALAD DRESSING *1–2 small red chilies, finely chopped* ‖ *3 tablespoons lime or lemon juice* ‖ *1 tablespoon fish sauce*

ONE Make the dressing. Mix all ingredients together in a small bowl. This can be done 1–2 hours ahead. **TWO** Bring a saucepan of water to a boil. Add the chicken, boil for 5 minutes, and drain. Transfer the chicken to a mixing bowl and let cool, then tear into long, thin threads. **THREE** Slice the cucumber, discard the seeds, and grate the flesh into long, thin shreds; mix with the chicken. **FOUR** Add the shallots, roasted peanuts, and salad dressing; combine well. Garnish with a few cilantro leaves before serving.

Serves 4 with 2 other main dishes

NUTRIENT ANALYSIS PER SERVING 339 kJ – 80 cal – 10 g protein – 4 g carbohydrate – 2 g sugars – 3 g fat – 1 g saturated fat – 1 g fiber – 240 mg sodium

HEALTHY TIP Low in saturated fat, cholesterol, and sodium, cucumber is a good source of silica, which helps build healthy connective tissue. Cucumber also contains plenty of dietary fiber, together with the water you need when ingesting fiber, plus various trace elements such as copper and manganese.

Spicy sliced steak

When Thai men get together to drink, they love to eat this dish, which comes from the north of Thailand. It can be quite hot, but you can adjust the amount of chili to suit your taste.

INGREDIENTS *12 oz rump, sirloin, or fillet steak* ‖ *1 lemongrass stalk (white part only), 5 inches long, finely sliced* ‖ *3 shallots, finely sliced* ‖ *5 kaffir lime leaves, finely sliced* ‖ *4 tablespoons lemon juice* ‖ *1½ tablespoons fish sauce* ‖ *1 tablespoon ground rice (see page 10)* ‖ *3–4 small red or green chilies, finely chopped, or ½–1 teaspoon chili powder (or to taste)* ‖ *2 tablespoons mint leaves, roughly chopped* ‖ *mixed salad leaves*

ONE Preheat the grill or broiler to medium. If you are using the broiler, line the tray with foil. Put the beef on the grill rack and cook for 5–7 minutes on each side, turning occasionally. Let the meat rest for at least 5 minutes, then slice crosswise into strips. **TWO** In a bowl, mix together the beef, lemongrass, shallots, kaffir lime leaves, lemon juice, fish sauce, ground rice, chilies or chili powder, and mint leaves. **THREE** Line a serving plate with a few mixed salad leaves and top with the sliced steak. Serve immediately.

Serves 4 with 3 other main dishes

NUTRIENT ANALYSIS PER SERVING 694 kJ – 166 cal – 21 g protein – 7 g carbohydrate – 1 g sugars – 6 g fat – 3 g saturated fat – 0 g fiber – 360 mg sodium

HEALTHY TIP Few foods are as healthy as fresh salad. For maximum benefit, use Romaine lettuce for its high fiber content, vitamin C, beta-carotene, and folic acid.

Grilled squid salad with cashews

Mangoes and cashews are united here in this delicious grilled squid salad.

INGREDIENTS *2 lb squid* ‖ *1 small green mango or cooking apple, peeled and finely shredded* ‖ *2 medium carrots, finely shredded* ‖ *6 shallots, finely sliced* ‖ *¼ cup roasted cashews* ‖ *Romaine lettuce leaves* ‖ *cilantro leaves, to garnish*

SALAD DRESSING *3–4 small red and green chilies, finely chopped* ‖ *5 tablespoons lime or lemon juice* ‖ *1½ tablespoons fish sauce*

ONE Make the dressing. Combine all ingredients in a small bowl. **TWO** Prepare the squid *(see page 12)*. Grill or broil the squid for 3–4 minutes on each side, turning occasionally, until cooked through. Remove the squid from the heat, transfer to a mixing bowl, and let cool. **THREE** Mix the mango, carrots, shallots, and salad dressing with the squid and combine well. **FOUR** Line a serving plate with lettuce leaves and top with the squid. Sprinkle with the cashews, garnish with cilantro leaves, and serve immediately.

Serves 4 with 3 other main dishes

NUTRIENT ANALYSIS PER SERVING 1250 kJ – 299 cal – 40 g protein – 13 g carbohydrate – 7 g sugars – 8 g fat – 1 g saturated fat – 1 g fiber – 460 mg sodium

HEALTHY TIP Cashews are a good source of copper, magnesium, zinc, and biotin. Magnesium balances the effects of calcium and helps regulate nerve and muscle tone.

Shrimp salad

There is a lovely aroma from the kaffir lime leaves in this healthy and popular dish. Its attractive appearance makes it ideal for parties.

INGREDIENTS *14½ oz raw shrimp, large- or medium-sized* ‖ *2 lemongrass stalks (white part only), each 5 inches long, finely sliced* ‖ *2 garlic cloves, finely sliced* ‖ *3 kaffir lime leaves, finely sliced* ‖ *mixed salad leaves* ‖ *mint leaves, to garnish*

SALAD DRESSING *1–2 small red chilies, finely chopped* ‖ *5 tablespoons lime or lemon juice* ‖ *1 tablespoon fish sauce*

ONE Make the dressing. Combine all ingredients in a small bowl. **TWO** Prepare the shrimp *(see page 12)*. Cook the shrimp in boiling water for 2 minutes, drain, and let cool in a mixing bowl. **THREE** Add the lemongrass, garlic, kaffir lime leaves, and salad dressing, and toss. **FOUR** Line a serving plate with mixed salad leaves and top with the shrimp salad. Garnish with a few mint leaves and serve immediately.

Serves 4 as a starter

NUTRIENT ANALYSIS PER SERVING 266 kJ – 63 cal – 11 g protein – 3 g carbohydrate – 1 g sugars – 1 g fat – 0 g saturated fat – 1 g fiber – 900 mg sodium

HEALTHY TIP Although shrimp contain cholesterol, they have virtually no saturated fat, which makes them a good choice as part of a low-fat diet.

Hot and sour vermicelli with shrimp

This is a tangy version of a noodle salad. Vermicelli, or *wun sen* noodles, are made from mung beans, and they become nearly transparent when they have been soaked in hot water.

INGREDIENTS *6 oz large raw shrimp* ‖ *4 oz mung bean vermicelli noodles* ‖ *½ oz dried black fungus* ‖ *3 tablespoons lime or lemon juice* ‖ *1 tablespoon fish sauce* ‖ *2 lemongrass stalks (white part only), each 5 inches long, finely sliced* ‖ *3 shallots, finely sliced* ‖ *¼–½ teaspoon chili powder or 2–3 small red and green chilies, finely sliced (or to taste)* ‖ *3 green onions, finely chopped* ‖ *mixed salad leaves* ‖ *mint or cilantro leaves, to garnish*

ONE Prepare the shrimp *(see page 12)*. Soak the noodles in hot water for 1–2 minutes or until soft. Drain and roughly chop. Soak the dried black fungus in hot water for 2–3 minutes or until soft. Drain and roughly chop. **TWO** In a saucepan or wok, cook the shrimp, lime or lemon juice, and fish sauce over medium heat for 1–2 minutes or until shrimp open and turn pink. **THREE** Add the noodles and dried black fungus and cook for another 2 minutes or until noodles are cooked. Remove from heat. **FOUR** Add the lemongrass, shallots, chili powder or chilies, and green onions and mix well. Line a serving plate with mixed salad leaves and top with the seafood mixture. Garnish with a few mint or cilantro leaves and serve immediately.

Serves 4 with 2 other main dishes

NUTRIENT ANALYSIS PER SERVING 640 kJ – 153 cal – 8 g protein – 29 g carbohydrate – 1g sugars – 1 g fat – 0 g saturated fat – 0 g fiber – 480 mg sodium

HEALTHY TIP Shrimp are an excellent source of protein and a great way to get iron, zinc, and vitamin E. They have virtually no saturated fat.

Quail egg salad with steamed shrimp

Tiny quail eggs and shrimp are an attractive combination, especially when they are combined with shredded mango and a delicious salad dressing.

INGREDIENTS *4 oz raw shrimp, large- or medium-sized* ‖ *24 quail eggs* ‖ *1 small mango or cooking apple, peeled and finely shredded* ‖ *2 garlic cloves, finely chopped* ‖ *4 shallots, finely sliced* ‖ *mixed salad leaves* ‖ *1 long red chili, stemmed, seeded, and finely sliced, to garnish*

SALAD DRESSING *1–2 small red and green chilies, finely chopped* ‖ *4 tablespoons lime or lemon juice* ‖ *1½ tablespoons light soy sauce*

ONE Make the dressing. Combine all ingredients in a small bowl. **TWO** Prepare the shrimp *(see page 12)*. **THREE** Fill a wok or steamer pan with water. Position the bamboo steamer basket or steamer rack in the pan, cover, and bring the water to a boil over medium heat. Taking care not to burn your hand, gently place all the quail eggs into the steamer basket and steam for 6–8 minutes. Pour in cool water, shell the eggs, halve them lengthwise with a sharp knife, and put them in a bowl. **FOUR** Place the shrimp on a plate that will fit inside the steamer basket, cover, and steam for 2 minutes. Remove the shrimp and add them to the quail eggs. **FIVE** Add the mango, garlic, shallots, and salad dressing and toss well. **SIX** Line a serving plate with mixed salad leaves and top with the egg salad. Garnish with the finely chopped chili and serve immediately.

Serves 4 with 3 other main dishes

NUTRIENT ANALYSIS PER SERVING 684 kJ – 163 cal – 14 g protein – 8 g carbohydrate – 7 g sugars – 9 g fat – 2 g saturated fat – 2 g fiber – 190 mg sodium

HEALTHY TIP Mangoes are rich in vitamins, minerals, and antioxidants, high in fiber, and low in calories and sodium. They are a good source of vitamin A and also contain vitamins B and C as well as potassium, calcium, and iron.

Grilled fish salad

Try to obtain perfectly fresh fish for this main dish, which often appears on a family menu. If you want to make it hotter, just add extra chili.

INGREDIENTS *2 mackerel or whiting, cleaned and gutted, with or without heads, with a total weight of 13 oz* ‖ *2 lemongrass stalks (white part only), each 5 inches long, finely sliced* ‖ *3 shallots, finely sliced* ‖ *1 inch fresh ginger root, peeled and finely sliced* ‖ *5 kaffir lime leaves, finely sliced* ‖ *1 oz mint leaves* ‖ *¼ cup lime or lemon juice* ‖ *1 tablespoon fish sauce* ‖ *3–4 small red and green chilies, finely sliced* ‖ *mixed salad leaves* ‖ *1 long red chili, stemmed, seeded, and finely chopped, to garnish*

ONE Grill the fish over medium heat for about 20 minutes on each side or until cooked and lightly browned. (You can place the fish in a fish-shaped griddle that opens out on a hinge. The fish are sandwiched in between and are easier to lift and turn on the grill.) **TWO** When the fish have slightly cooled, remove the heads, spines, and other bones with your hands and discard. Break all the fish, including the skin, into bite-sized chunks and place in a bowl. **THREE** Add the lemongrass, shallots, ginger, kaffir lime leaves, mint leaves, lime or lemon juice, fish sauce, and chilies and gently mix the ingredients together. **FOUR** Line a serving plate with mixed salad leaves and top with the fish mixture. Garnish with the chili and serve immediately.

Serves 4 with 2 other main dishes

NUTRIENT ANALYSIS PER SERVING 1015 kJ – 244 cal – 20 g protein – 4 g carbohydrate – 1 g sugars – 17g fat – 3 g saturated fat – 0 g fiber – 34 mg sodium

HEALTHY TIP Fish is a good source of omega-3 polyunsaturated fatty acids, and most nutritionists believe fish should be on everyone's menu at least once a week.

Rice flake salad

Rice flake noodles are more often used in soups than in salads, but this dish is an exception: a spicy noodle salad.

INGREDIENTS *1 lb boneless, skinless chicken breasts* ‖ *1 lb raw shrimp, large- or medium- sized* ‖ *16 oz rice flake (kua chap) noodles* ‖ *8 shallots, finely sliced* ‖ *2–3 green onions, finely chopped* ‖ *mixed salad leaves* ‖ *cilantro leaves, to garnish*

SALAD DRESSING *3–4 small red chilies, finely chopped* ‖ *⅔ cup lime or lemon juice* ‖ *2 tablespoons fish sauce*

ONE Make the dressing. Combine all ingredients in a small bowl. **TWO** Prepare the shrimp *(see page 12)*. **THREE** Cook the chicken in a large pot of boiling water for 6–7 minutes or until cooked. Remove the chicken from the boiling water and set aside to cool. Tear the chicken into long, thin threads. **FOUR** Cook the shrimp in the same boiling water for 2 minutes, then lift them out and add to the chicken threads. **FIVE** Gently drop the noodles into the remaining boiling water and cook for 2–3 minutes or until cooked and soft. Drain the noodles and run under cold water. Drain again and add to the chicken and shrimp. **SIX** Add the shallots, green onions, and salad dressing and combine well. Line a serving plate with a few mixed salad leaves and top with the rice flake salad. Garnish with a few cilantro leaves and serve immediately.

Serves 4 with 2 other main dishes

NUTRIENT ANALYSIS PER SERVING 2834 kJ – 676 cal – 45 g protein – 108 g carbohydrate – 3 g sugars – 5 g fat – 2 g saturated fat – 1 g fiber – 1290 mg sodium

HEALTHY TIP Rice noodles are completely gluten-free, which makes them an attractive option for people with wheat allergies who cannot eat gluten.

Spicy seafood salad

Finely sliced ginger is a perfect combination with seafood. Ideal for people on a diet, this dish can be eaten on its own or as a side salad.

INGREDIENTS *1 lb mixed seafood, such as shrimp, squid, and small scallops* ‖ *¼ cup lime or lemon juice* ‖ *1 tablespoon fish sauce* ‖ *2 lemongrass stalks (white part only), each 5 inches long, finely sliced* ‖ *3 shallots, finely sliced* ‖ *1 inch fresh ginger root, peeled and finely sliced* ‖ *3–4 small red or green chilies, finely chopped, or ½–1 teaspoon chili powder (or to taste)* ‖ *2 tablespoons finely chopped mint leaves* ‖ *mixed salad leaves* ‖ *mint leaves, to garnish*

ONE Prepare the mixed seafood *(see page 12)*, cutting the squid into rings, rather than scoring it. **TWO** In a saucepan or wok, cook the mixed seafood with the lime or lemon juice and fish sauce over medium heat for 2–3 minutes or until the shrimp open and turn pink and all the seafood is cooked. **THREE** Stir in the lemongrass, shallots, ginger, chilies, and mint leaves and mix well. **FOUR** Line a serving plate with mixed salad leaves and top with the seafood. Garnish with a few mint leaves and serve immediately.

Serves 4 with 3 other main dishes

NUTRIENT ANALYSIS PER SERVING 500 kJ – 119 cal – 20 g protein – 5 g carbohydrate – 1 g sugars – 0 g fat – 0 g saturated fat – 0 g fiber – 600 mg sodium

HEALTHY TIP A balanced combination of seafood, fresh herbs, and salad is one of the healthiest low-fat dishes you can prepare.

Pomelo and shrimp salad

This is an ideal dish for a hot, sunny day. Pomelo is wonderfully refreshing, and its flesh has a unique, crumbly texture that melts in your mouth. When mixed with other ingredients in a salad, its slightly sour taste enhances the taste of the dish. Pomelo salad can be made with cooked meats such as chicken or pork, or, as here, with shrimp. After peeling the pomelo you should be left with about 1½ lb of flesh. If you can't find pomelo, use grapefruit instead.

INGREDIENTS *2½ lb pomelo* ‖ *8 oz raw shrimp* ‖ *3 oz shallots, finely sliced* ‖ *1 tablespoon roughly torn cilantro leaves* ‖ *½ long chili, finely chopped* ‖ *1½ tablespoons fish sauce* ‖ *1½ tablespoons shredded dried coconut* ‖ *cilantro leaves, to garnish*

ONE Peel the pomelo *(see page 11)* and crumble the segments into their component parts, without squashing them or releasing the juice. **TWO** Prepare the shrimp *(see page 12)*. **THREE** Cook the shrimp in boiling water for 2 minutes and drain. Transfer to a mixing bowl and let cool. **FOUR** Add the pomelo to the shrimp and gently combine with the shallots, cilantro leaves, chili, and fish sauce. Sprinkle with shredded coconut *(see page 11)*, garnish with a few cilantro leaves, and serve immediately. If the pomelo is not sour (taste it!) add 3–4 tablespoons of lemon juice to provide a slightly sour taste.

Serves 4 as a starter

NUTRIENT ANALYSIS PER SERVING 487 kJ – 116 cal – 7 g protein – 16 g carbohydrate – 14 g sugars – 3g fat – 2 g saturated fat – 3 g fiber – 615 mg sodium

HEALTHY TIP A relative of the grapefruit, pomelo is rich in vitamin C and potassium.

Fish and seafood

Grilled fish with three-flavor sauce

You can vary the sauce served with this dish, using lemon juice for a clear sauce with a sharp taste or tamarind pulp for a thicker, darker sauce with a smooth, sour taste.

INGREDIENTS *1 red snapper or sea bream, about 14½ oz* ‖ *3 garlic cloves, roughly chopped* ‖ *3 shallots, roughly chopped* ‖ *5 long red chilies, seeded and roughly chopped* ‖ *3 cilantro roots, roughly chopped* ‖ *2 tablespoons sunflower oil, divided* ‖ *2 tablespoons Vegetable Stock (see page 16) or water* ‖ *2 tablespoons lemon juice* ‖ *1½ tablespoons fish sauce* ‖ *2 tablespoons palm or coconut sugar* ‖ *Thai sweet basil leaves, to garnish*

ONE Prepare the fish *(see page 12)*. **TWO** Use a mortar and pestle or small blender to combine the garlic, shallots, chilies, and cilantro roots into a rough paste. **THREE** Rub the outside of the fish with ½ tablespoon oil and grill it over medium heat for 15–20 minutes on each side or until the fish is cooked and lightly browned. (You can place the fish in a fish-shaped griddle that opens out on a hinge. The fish is sandwiched between the griddle and is easier to lift and turn on the grill.) Transfer the fish to a serving plate and keep warm. **FOUR** Heat the remaining oil in a nonstick wok or skillet and stir-fry the garlic and chili paste over medium heat for 2 minutes or until fragrant. Add the stock, lemon juice, fish sauce, and sugar and cook for another minute or until the sugar has dissolved. **FIVE** Pour the chili sauce over the warm fish, garnish with a few Thai sweet basil leaves, and serve immediately.

Serves 4 with 3 other main dishes

NUTRIENT ANALYSIS PER SERVING 933 kJ – 222 cal – 21 g protein – 15 g carbohydrate – 11 g sugars – 9 g fat – 1 g saturated fat – 0 g fiber – 600 mg sodium

HEALTHY TIP Studies have shown that chilies may help reduce blood cholesterol levels. Some reports indicate that eating chilies can help ward off gastric ulcers. They cause the stomach lining to secrete a mucus that coats and protects it from damage by irritants such as alcohol.

Stir-fried crab with vermicelli

Clear noodles are essential for stir-frying with crab. I remember eating this dish as a child because my father always ordered it when we went on trips to the seaside. Children eat the noodles; grown-ups eat the crab.

INGREDIENTS *1 lb fresh crab* ‖ *4 oz mung bean vermicelli noodles* ‖ *1½ tablespoons sunflower oil* ‖ *3 garlic cloves, finely chopped* ‖ *3 tablespoons Seafood Stock (see page 16) or water* ‖ *1 small onion, quartered* ‖ *½ red bell pepper, finely diced* ‖ *1 small carrot, cut into thin strips* ‖ *1 inch fresh ginger root, peeled and finely sliced* ‖ *1 tablespoon oyster sauce* ‖ *1 tablespoon light soy sauce* ‖ *2 green onions, finely sliced* ‖ *cilantro leaves, to garnish*

ONE Prepare the crab *(see page 12)*. Soak the noodles in hot water for 2–3 minutes, or until soft, then drain and roughly chop. **TWO** Heat the oil in a nonstick wok or skillet and stir-fry the garlic over medium heat until lightly browned. **THREE** Add the crab pieces and stock or water and stir-fry for 8–10 minutes or until the crab is cooked. **FOUR** Add the noodles and all the remaining ingredients and stir-fry for another 3–4 minutes. Spoon onto a serving plate, garnish with a few cilantro leaves, and serve immediately.

Serves 4 with 2 other main dishes

NUTRIENT ANALYSIS PER SERVING 839 kJ – 200 cal – 9 g protein – 29 g carbohydrate – 3 g sugars – 6 g fat – 1 g saturated fat – 1 g fiber – 300 mg sodium

HEALTHY TIP Low in fat, crab meat is high in omega-3 fatty acids. It is also rich in zinc, which boosts the immune system.

Fish with ginger sauce

This broiled or grilled dish is another way of enjoying the combination of fish and ginger. Eat it at a main meal or alongside a soup or any curry or stir-fried dish.

INGREDIENTS *14–16 oz red snapper, gray mullet, plaice, or lemon sole* ‖ *less than ¼ oz dried black fungus* ‖ *2 tablespoons sunflower oil, divided* ‖ *3–4 garlic cloves, finely chopped* ‖ *1 small carrot, finely sliced* ‖ *2 oz fresh ginger root, peeled and finely sliced* ‖ *2 tablespoons Vegetable or Seafood Stock (see page 16) or water* ‖ *1 tablespoon oyster sauce* ‖ *1 tablespoon light soy sauce*

TO SERVE *2 green onions, finely sliced diagonally* ‖ *cilantro leaves*

ONE Prepare the fish *(see page 12)*. Soak the dried black fungus in hot water for 2–3 minutes or until soft. Drain and roughly chop. **TWO** Rub the outside of the fish with ½ tablespoon oil and grill over medium heat for 15–20 minutes on each side until cooked and lightly browned. (You can place the fish in a fish-shaped griddle that opens out on a hinge. The fish is sandwiched in between the griddle and is easier to lift and turn on the grill.) Transfer the fish to a serving plate and keep warm. **THREE** Heat the remaining oil in a nonstick wok or skillet and stir-fry the garlic over medium heat until lightly browned. **FOUR** Add the carrots, ginger, dried black fungus, and the remaining ingredients and stir-fry for another 3–4 minutes. Pour the stir-fried mixture over the warm fish, garnish with the green onions and a few cilantro leaves, and serve immediately.

Serves 4 with 3 other main dishes

NUTRIENT ANALYSIS PER SERVING 670 kJ – 160 cal – 20 g protein – 4 g carbohydrate – 1g sugars – 7 g fat – 1 g saturated fat – 0 g fiber – 320 mg sodium

HEALTHY TIP Ginger is known to be one of the best herbs for digestion, and it also improves and stimulates the circulation of blood throughout the body. It relieves nausea and lowers bad (LDL) cholesterol.

Garlic shrimp

Only Thais use cilantro roots in cooking, and if you can obtain them you'll see why we do. This is one of the best ways of stir-frying shrimp and creates a very sophisticated dish.

INGREDIENTS *1 lb raw large- or medium-sized shrimp* ‖ *5 garlic cloves, roughly chopped* ‖ *15 cilantro roots, roughly chopped* ‖ *10 black peppercorns* ‖ *1½ tablespoons sunflower oil* ‖ *2 tablespoons Vegetable or Seafood Stock (see page 16) or water* ‖ *1 tablespoon oyster sauce* ‖ *1 tablespoon light soy sauce* ‖ *cilantro leaves, to garnish*

ONE Prepare the shrimp *(see page 12)*. **TWO** Use a mortar and pestle to grind the garlic and cilantro roots into a rough paste. Add the peppercorns and continue to grind roughly. **THREE** Heat the oil in a nonstick wok or skillet and stir-fry the garlic paste over medium heat for 1–2 minutes or until fragrant. **FOUR** Add the shrimp, stock, oyster sauce, and soy sauce; stir-fry for another 2–3 minutes or until shrimp open and turn pink. Garnish with a few cilantro leaves and serve immediately.

Serves 4 with 3 other main dishes

NUTRIENT ANALYSIS PER SERVING 458 kJ – 110 cal – 11 g protein – 2 g carbohydrate – 0 g sugars – 6 g fat – 1 g saturated fat – 0 g fiber – 1030 mg sodium

HEALTHY TIP Garlic contains allicin, which has antifungal and antibiotic properties. It also has other compounds that have been shown to make carcinogens inactive and suppress the growth of tumors.

Seafood curry steamed in banana leaves

This curried seafood custard can also be made with fish or meat if you prefer. Steaming in handmade banana cups with basil leaves creates a beautiful aroma, but if you cannot find banana leaves, use small ovenproof bowls instead.

INGREDIENTS *about 3 long banana leaves* ‖ *6 dried, long red chilies, each about 5 inches long* ‖ *5 garlic cloves, roughly chopped* ‖ *4 shallots, roughly chopped* ‖ *5 cilantro roots, roughly chopped* ‖ *1 lemongrass stalk (white part only), 5 inches long, finely sliced* ‖ *1 inch fresh galangal, peeled and finely sliced* ‖ *3 kaffir lime leaves, finely sliced* ‖ *1 teaspoon shrimp paste* ‖ *¾ cup canned coconut milk, shaken well; reserve 2 tablespoons for garnish* ‖ *1¼ cups Seafood Stock (see page 16)* ‖ *4 eggs* ‖ *3 tablespoons fish sauce* ‖ *15 oz mixed seafood, such as white fish fillet cut into ½ inch pieces, small shrimp, scallops, and squid* ‖ *2 oz Thai sweet basil leaves* ‖ *1 long red chili, stemmed, seeded, and finely sliced, to garnish*

ONE Blanch the banana leaves in hot water for 1–2 minutes to soften them and prevent them from splitting. **TWO** Cut the leaves into 20 circles, 6 inches across; place 2 pieces of banana leaf on top of each other, the bottom leaf with the fiber running lengthwise, the top leaf with the fiber running across. Make a ½ inch tuck about 1½ inches deep and pin it securely with a small toothpick. Repeat this at the opposite point and at the two side points. You will now have 10 square cups with flat bases. **THREE** Stem and slit the chilies with a sharp knife; seed and roughly chop the flesh. Soak the chilies in hot water for 2 minutes or until soft, then drain. **FOUR** Use a mortar and pestle or blender to grind the chilies, garlic, and shallots into a paste. Add the cilantro roots, lemongrass, galangal, kaffir lime leaves, and shrimp paste and pound until the mixture forms a smooth paste. **FIVE** Combine the curry paste, coconut milk, stock, eggs, fish sauce, and mixed seafood. **SIX** Place a few basil leaves in the bottom of each banana cup and spoon in the fish mixture until the cups are three-quarters full. **SEVEN** Place each cup on a plate that will fit inside a bamboo steamer or steamer rack and steam for 10–15 minutes. Check and replenish the water every 10 minutes. Three minutes before the end of cooking time, spoon a little of the reserved coconut milk onto each cup with a few slices of the chili. Serve hot or warm.

Makes 10 banana cups; serves 4 with 2 other main dishes

NUTRIENT ANALYSIS PER SERVING 1229 kJ – 294 cal – 30 g protein – 8 g carbohydrate – 2 g sugars – 16 g fat – 8 g saturated fat – 0 g fiber – 1340 mg sodium

HEALTHY TIP Always use fresh fish—it is easier to smell whether fish is fresh if it is not prewrapped in a plastic container.

Steamed mussels with lemongrass

You can steam clams in exactly the same way as described here or, if you prefer, you can mix mussels and clams together to make this popular dish. Serve with Chili and Lime Sauce *(see page 21)*.

INGREDIENTS *2 lb mussels in their shells* ‖ *1½ tablespoons sunflower oil* ‖ *4 garlic cloves, finely chopped* ‖ *3 lemongrass stalks, cut into 1 inch lengths* ‖ *1½ inches galangal, peeled and cut into 7–8 slices* ‖ *1½ tablespoons fish sauce* ‖ *1½ tablespoons lemon juice* ‖ *2 long red chilies, stemmed, seeded, and finely chopped* ‖ *Thai sweet basil leaves, roughly chopped*

ONE Prepare the mussels *(see page 12)*. **TWO** Heat the oil in a nonstick wok or skillet and stir-fry the garlic, lemongrass, and galangal over medium heat for 2–3 minutes or until fragrant. **THREE** Add the mussels to the wok and stir-fry for a few minutes. Add the fish sauce and lemon juice, loosely cover with a lid, and cook over medium heat for 10–15 minutes, shaking the pan frequently. **FOUR** Cook until the mussels open, discarding any shells that have not opened. Add the chilies and a few chopped basil leaves; mix together lightly before serving in a large bowl.

Serves 4 with 3 other main dishes

NUTRIENT ANALYSIS PER SERVING 490 kJ – 117 cal – 14 g protein – 2 g carbohydrate – 0 g sugars – 6 g fat – 1 g saturated fat – 0 g fiber – 420 mg sodium

HEALTHY TIP Although mussels do not provide omega-3 fatty acids, they are an excellent source of selenium and vitamin B12 and are a good source of zinc and folate.

Stir-fried scallops with baby bok choi

The orange of the scallop corals contrasts beautifully with the green of the baby bok choi to create a colorful, crunchy dish.

INGREDIENTS *10 oz scallops, including the corals* ∥ *1½ tablespoons sunflower oil* ∥ *3 garlic cloves, finely chopped* ∥ *10 oz baby bok choi* ∥ *1 tablespoon oyster sauce*

ONE Prepare the scallops *(see page 12)*. **TWO** Heat the oil in a nonstick wok or skillet and stir-fry the garlic over medium heat until lightly browned. Add the scallops and stir-fry for 1–2 minutes. **THREE** Add the baby bok choi and oyster sauce, stir-fry for another 2–3 minutes, and serve immediately.

Serves 4 with 3 other main dishes

NUTRIENT ANALYSIS PER SERVING 722 kJ – 172 cal – 22 g protein – 7 g carbohydrate – 0 g sugars – 7 g fat – 1 g saturated fat – 0 g fiber – 360 mg sodium

HEALTHY TIP Dark green, leafy vegetables such as bok choi provide a lot of vitamin C, as well as vitamin B6, folate, and niacin.

Black sesame seeds with shrimp and water chestnuts

Black sesame seeds are popular ingredients in Thai recipes because of their health-giving properties. This recipe combines them with the interesting textures of shrimps and water chestnuts.

INGREDIENTS *8 oz shrimp* ‖ *½ tablespoon black sesame seeds* ‖ *1½ tablespoons sunflower oil* ‖ *2–3 garlic cloves, finely chopped* ‖ *7 oz canned water chestnuts, drained and thinly sliced* ‖ *4 oz snow peas, trimmed* ‖ *2 tablespoons Vegetable or Seafood Stock (see page 16) or water* ‖ *1 tablespoon light soy sauce* ‖ *1 tablespoon oyster sauce*

ONE Prepare the shrimp *(see page 12)*. **TWO** Dry-fry the black sesame seeds in a small pan for 1–2 minutes or until fragrant; set aside. **THREE** Heat the oil in a nonstick wok or skillet and stir-fry the garlic over medium heat until lightly browned. **FOUR** Add the shrimp, water chestnuts, and snow peas and stir-fry over high heat for 1–2 minutes. Add the stock and remaining ingredients and stir-fry for another 2–3 minutes or until the shrimp open and turn pink. Stir in the fried sesame seeds and serve immediately.

Serves 4 with 2 other main dishes

NUTRIENT ANALYSIS PER SERVING 488 kJ – 117 cal – 8 g protein – 9 g carbohydrate – 1 g sugars – 6 g fat – 1 g saturated fat – 1 g fiber – 550 mg sodium

HEALTHY TIP A very good source of calcium, black sesame seeds also have high amounts of protein, phosphorus, iron, and magnesium. They can ease constipation and promote regular bowel movements.

Red curry with fish and tofu

This recipe uses white fish fillets such as cod or swordfish that retain their texture after being ground and pounded into a smooth paste. They go very well with tofu.

INGREDIENTS *10 oz white fish fillets, skinned and roughly chopped* ‖ *3 garlic cloves, roughly chopped* ‖ *3 cilantro roots, finely chopped* ‖ *¼ teaspoon ground white pepper* ‖ *1½ tablespoons cornstarch* ‖ *1½ tablespoons sunflower oil* ‖ *1 recipe Red Curry Paste (see page 18) or 1–2 oz purchased red curry paste* ‖ *¾ cup canned coconut milk, shaken well* ‖ *¾ cup Vegetable or Seafood Stock (see page 16)* ‖ *2 tablespoons fish sauce* ‖ *1½ tablespoons palm or coconut sugar* ‖ *7 oz firm tofu, cut into 1 inch cubes* ‖ *5 kaffir lime leaves, torn in half*

TO SERVE *Thai sweet basil leaves* ‖ *2 long red chilies, stemmed, seeded, and finely sliced*

ONE Blend together the fish fillets, garlic, cilantro roots, ground white pepper, and cornstarch in a food processor or blender to make a smooth paste. Spoon into a bowl. **TWO** Heat the oil in a nonstick wok or skillet and stir-fry the red curry paste over medium heat for 2 minutes or until fragrant. **THREE** Add the coconut milk and stock. With a spoon or your wet fingers, shape the fish paste into small balls or discs, about ¾ inch across, and gently drop into the hot but not boiling coconut milk. Continue until you have used up the fish. **FOUR** Add the fish sauce and sugar and cook for another 5 minutes, stirring occasionally. **FIVE** Add the tofu cubes and cook for 1–2 minutes, taking care not to let the tofu cubes lose their shape. Add the kaffir lime leaves. Spoon into a serving bowl, garnish with Thai sweet basil leaves and chilies, and serve immediately.

Serves 4 with 2 other main dishes

NUTRIENT ANALYSIS PER SERVING 1299 kJ – 311 cal – 21 g protein – 21 g carbohydrate – 11 g sugars – 16 g fat – 7 g saturated fat – 1 g fiber – 720 mg sodium

HEALTHY TIP Fish is a good source of niacin and vitamin B12, selenium, and pantothenic acid; the latter is essential for growth and reproduction.

Green-flowering chives with squid

More fibrous in texture than either green onions or true chives, Chinese chives are available in "leafy" and "flowering" types. This dish uses the tender stems of the green-flowering chives, available at Asian stores.

INGREDIENTS *1 lb squid* ‖ *1½ tablespoons sunflower oil* ‖ *4 garlic cloves, finely chopped* ‖ *2 tablespoons Vegetable or Seafood Stock (see page 16) or water* ‖ *1 tablespoon light soy sauce* ‖ *1½ tablespoons oyster sauce* ‖ *12 oz Chinese flowering chives, cut into 2 inch lengths (discard the hard ends of the stems)* ‖ *ground white pepper*

ONE Prepare the squid *(see page 12)*. **TWO** Heat the oil in a nonstick wok or skillet and stir-fry the garlic over medium heat until lightly browned. Add the squid, stock, soy sauce, oyster sauce, and chives and stir-fry for 2–3 minutes or until all are cooked. Season with ground white pepper.

Serves 4 with 2 other main dishes

NUTRIENT ANALYSIS PER SERVING 682 kJ – 163 cal – 22 g protein – 4 g carbohydrate – 2 g sugars – 6 g fat – 1 g saturated fat – 0 g fiber – 535 mg sodium

HEALTHY TIP In Asia, Chinese chives traditionally have been used as an herbal medicine to aid recovery from fatigue. They are a good source of vitamins A and C.

Scallop curry with mango

You need to select just the right mango for this dish: not too ripe and soft, but not too green and sour. It should be firm to the touch but not hard and just turning from green to yellow-orange. With the right mango, it's a delicious combination.

INGREDIENTS *15 oz scallops, including the corals* ‖ *1½ tablespoons sunflower oil* ‖ *1 recipe Dry Curry Paste (see page 19) or 1–2 oz purchased dry curry paste* ‖ *½ cup coconut milk, shaken well* ‖ *½ cup Vegetable or Seafood Stock (see page 16) or water* ‖ *1 tablespoon fish sauce* ‖ *1 tablespoon palm or coconut sugar* ‖ *7 oz half-ripe mango, peeled, pitted, and cut into bite-sized pieces*

TO SERVE *Thai sweet basil leaves* ‖ *1 long red chili, stemmed, seeded, and finely sliced*

ONE Prepare the scallops *(see page 12)*. **TWO** Heat the oil in a nonstick wok or skillet and stir-fry the dry curry paste over medium heat for 2 minutes or until fragrant. **THREE** Add the coconut milk, stock, fish sauce, and sugar and bring to a boil. **FOUR** Add the scallops and mango and cook for 3–4 minutes or until the scallops are cooked to your liking. Spoon into a serving bowl, garnish with Thai sweet basil leaves and the chili, and serve immediately.

Serves 4 with 2 other main dishes

NUTRIENT ANALYSIS PER SERVING 1285 kJ – 305 cal – 30 g protein – 22 g carbohydrate – 14 g sugars – 11 g fat – 4 g saturated fat – 2 g fiber – 550 mg sodium

HEALTHY TIP Scallops are a very good source of protein, vitamin B12, omega-3 fatty acids, magnesium, and potassium.

Salmon fillets with chili and ginger
Although salmon is not native to Thailand, it is a convenient substitute for indigenous Thai fish that are not available elsewhere.

INGREDIENTS *4 boneless salmon fillets, 4 oz each, skinned* ‖ *1 long red chili, stemmed, seeded, and finely sliced* ‖ *1½ inches fresh ginger root, peeled and finely sliced* ‖ *2 green onions, finely sliced* ‖ *1½ tablespoons light soy sauce* ‖ *1 tablespoon lime or lemon juice* ‖ *ground black pepper* ‖ *cilantro leaves, to garnish*

ONE Fill a wok or steamer pan with water. Place the bamboo steamer basket or steamer rack into it, cover and bring the water to a boil over high heat. **TWO** Place the fish fillets on a deep plate that will fit on the rack of a bamboo steamer basket. Taking care not to burn your hand, set the plate inside the steamer basket, cover, and simmer for 10 minutes. **THREE** Add the chili, ginger, and green onions and sprinkle with the soy sauce, lime or lemon juice, and ground black pepper. Garnish with a few cilantro leaves and serve immediately.

Serves 4 with 2 other main dishes

NUTRIENT ANALYSIS PER SERVING 999 kJ – 240 cal – 24 g protein – 2 g carbohydrate – 0 g sugars – 0 g fat – 3 g saturated fat – 0 g fiber – 125 mg sodium

HEALTHY TIP You can get more than half your daily requirement of protein from a single portion of salmon. It is an excellent source of omega-3 fatty acids and contains less saturated fat than an equal amount of almost any other meat or poultry protein source.

Clams with ginger

One of my favorite dishes, seafood with the refreshing taste of ginger is a delightful combination. Be sure to provide a spare dish for the shells.

INGREDIENTS *2 lb clams in their shells* ‖ *2 tablespoons sunflower oil* ‖ *4–5 garlic cloves, finely chopped* ‖ *¼ cup Vegetable or Seafood Stock (see page 16) or water* ‖ *2 oz fresh ginger root, peeled and finely sliced* ‖ *1 tablespoon oyster sauce* ‖ *1 tablespoon light soy sauce* ‖ *2 green onions, finely sliced* ‖ *cilantro leaves, to garnish*

ONE Prepare the clams *(see page 12)*. **TWO** Heat the oil in a nonstick wok or skillet and stir-fry the garlic over medium heat until lightly browned. **THREE** Add the clams to the wok and stir-fry over medium heat for 4–5 minutes. Add the stock or water, ginger, oyster sauce, soy sauce, and green onions and stir-fry for another 2–3 minutes or until all the clams have opened. Discard any shells that have not opened. Spoon onto a serving plate, garnish with a few cilantro leaves, and serve immediately.

Serves 4 with 3 other main dishes

NUTRIENT ANALYSIS PER SERVING 558 kJ – 133 cal – 15 g protein – 3 g carbohydrate – 0 g sugars – 7 g fat – 1 g saturated fat – 0 g fiber – 380 mg sodium

HEALTHY TIP Very low in saturated fat, clams are high in omega-3 fatty acids, which are vital for the development and function of the brain as well as for lowering blood pressure.

Seafood with chilies

If you want a colorful stir-fry, try this recipe. There is no need to make it too hot, but you can add more chilies if you wish. Serve with Boiled Jasmine Rice *(see page 22).*

INGREDIENTS *14½ oz mixed seafood, such as shrimp, squid, small scallops, and white fish fillets (cod or sea bass)* ‖ *1½ tablespoons sunflower oil* ‖ *3–4 garlic cloves, finely chopped* ‖ *4 oz red bell pepper, seeded, and cut into bite-sized pieces* ‖ *1 small onion, cut into eighths* ‖ *1 carrot, cut into matchsticks* ‖ *1 inch fresh ginger root, peeled and finely sliced* ‖ *2 tablespoons Vegetable or Seafood Stock (see page 16) or water* ‖ *1 tablespoon oyster sauce* ‖ *½ tablespoon light soy sauce* ‖ *1 long red chili, stemmed, seeded, and sliced diagonally* ‖ *1–2 green onions, finely sliced*

ONE Prepare the mixed seafood *(see page 12).* **TWO** Heat the oil in a nonstick wok or skillet and stir-fry the garlic over medium heat until lightly browned. **THREE** Add the red bell pepper, onion, and carrots and stir-fry for 2 minutes. **FOUR** Add all the seafood together with the ginger, stock, oyster sauce, and soy sauce and stir-fry for 2–3 minutes or until the shrimp turn pink and all the seafood is cooked. **FIVE** Add the chili and green onions and mix well. Spoon onto a serving plate and serve immediately.

Serves 4 with 2 other main dishes

NUTRIENT ANALYSIS PER SERVING 697 kJ – 167 cal – 22 g protein – 7 g carbohydrate – 4 g sugars – 6 g fat – 1 g saturated fat – 1 g fiber – 720 mg sodium

HEALTHY TIP Chilies increase your metabolism and clear nasal congestion. They stimulate the circulation, act as a digestive aid, and have been shown to relieve many common ailments such as toothache.

Steamed fish with chili and lime juice

When you are steaming fish, it is useful to invest in a large wok and bamboo steamer basket or steamer rack. You can use two smaller fish if a large steamer is not easy to find.

INGREDIENTS *about 14½ oz pomfret, plaice, turbot, snapper, or sea bream* ‖ *3 garlic cloves, halved* ‖ *4 whole green onions, roots removed* ‖ *1 long red chili, seeded and finely chopped* ‖ *1½ tablespoons lime or lemon juice* ‖ *1 tablespoon light soy sauce* ‖ *ground white pepper*

ONE Prepare the fish *(see page 12)*. **TWO** Fill a wok or steamer pan with water, place the bamboo steamer basket or steamer rack into it, cover, and bring to a boil. **THREE** Place the fish on a deep plate that will fit on the rack of a bamboo steamer basket but that is slightly larger than the fish itself. **FOUR** Add the garlic and green onions and sprinkle over the chili, lime or lemon juice, and soy sauce. **FIVE** Taking care not to burn your hand, set the plate inside the steamer basket and simmer for 10 minutes. Season with ground white pepper and serve immediately.

Serves 4 with 3 other main dishes

NUTRIENT ANALYSIS PER SERVING 506 kJ – 120 cal – 21 g protein – 2 g carbohydrate – 0 g sugars – 3 g fat – 1 g saturated fat – 0 g fiber – 78 mg sodium

HEALTHY TIP Garlic's positive cardiovascular effects come partly from its sulfur compounds but also from its vitamin C, vitamin B6, selenium, and manganese content.

Meat and poultry

Chicken with mixed vegetables

There are lots of different vegetables in this dish. Choose them according to season and make sure they remain slightly crunchy. As always, the key to vegetable dishes is to avoid overcooking.

INGREDIENTS *11 oz mixed vegetables, including fresh baby corn, green beans, asparagus, and carrots* ‖ *1½ tablespoons sunflower oil* ‖ *3–4 garlic cloves, finely chopped* ‖ *11 oz boneless, skinless chicken breasts, cubed* ‖ *¼ cup Chicken Stock (see page 15), Vegetable Stock (see page 16), or water* ‖ *1 inch fresh ginger root, peeled and finely sliced* ‖ *2 tablespoons oyster sauce* ‖ *2 green onions, finely sliced* ‖ *cilantro leaves, to garnish*

ONE Prepare the vegetables. Cut the baby corn and green beans in half. Cut off the hard stems of the asparagus and slice each stalk into 2 inch lengths. Cut the carrots into matchsticks. **TWO** Blanch all the vegetables in boiling water for 30 seconds, remove, and plunge in a bowl of ice water to ensure a crispy texture, then drain. **THREE** Heat the oil in a nonstick wok or skillet and stir-fry the garlic over medium heat until lightly browned. **FOUR** Add the chicken and stir-fry for 3–5 minutes or until the meat is cooked. **FIVE** Add the mixed vegetables, stock, ginger, and oyster sauce and stir-fry for 2–3 minutes. Add the green onions. Spoon onto a serving plate and serve immediately.

Serves 4 with 2 other main dishes

NUTRIENT ANALYSIS PER SERVING 708 kJ – 169 cal – 20 g protein – 6 g carbohydrate – 4 g sugars – 7 g fat – 1 g saturated fat – 2 g fiber – 480 mg sodium

HEALTHY TIP Corn provides useful amounts of fiber and vitamin A (from beta-carotene).

Chicken with mixed mushrooms

If you use a selection of different types of mushrooms, this dish will have much more variety of texture and taste. You can use pork instead of chicken if you prefer.

INGREDIENTS *1½ tablespoons sunflower oil* ‖ *3 garlic cloves, finely chopped* ‖ *14½ oz boneless, skinless chicken breasts, thinly sliced* ‖ *9 oz mixed mushrooms, such as oyster, shiitake, button, and chestnut* ‖ *⅔ cup Chicken Stock (see page 15), Vegetable Stock (see page 16), or water* ‖ *1 inch fresh ginger root, peeled and finely sliced* ‖ *2 tablespoons oyster sauce* ‖ *2 green onions, finely sliced* ‖ *cilantro leaves, to garnish*

ONE Heat the oil in a nonstick wok or skillet and stir-fry the garlic over medium heat for 2 minutes or until lightly browned. **TWO** Add the chicken and stir-fry for 4–5 minutes. **THREE** Cut the mushrooms in half if they are large and remove and discard the hard stalks. Add the mushrooms, stock, ginger, and oyster sauce to the pan and stir-fry for another 3–5 minutes. Add the green onions and spoon onto a serving plate. Garnish with a few cilantro leaves and serve immediately.

Serves 4 with 2 other main dishes

NUTRIENT ANALYSIS PER SERVING 803 kJ – 190 cal – 27 g protein – 3 g carbohydrate – 0 g sugars – 8 g fat – 2 g saturated fat – 2 g fiber – 500 mg sodium

HEALTHY TIP Mushrooms provide useful amounts of some of the B vitamins as well as some of the trace mineral copper. A component of many enzymes, copper is needed for bone growth and for the formation of connective tissues.

Chicken with cashews
Thais and Westerners alike enjoy chicken with cashews. Stir-frying brings out a lovely aroma from the dried chili, making it one of our classics.

INGREDIENTS *1–2 dried, long red chilies, about 5 inches long* ‖ *1½ tablespoons sunflower oil, divided* ‖ *3 garlic cloves, finely chopped* ‖ *1 lb boneless, skinless chicken breasts, thinly sliced* ‖ *3 tablespoons Chicken Stock (see page 15), Vegetable Stock (see page 16), or water* ‖ *½ red bell pepper, seeded and cut into bite-sized pieces* ‖ *1 small carrot, cut into thin strips* ‖ *1 small onion, quartered* ‖ *1½ tablespoons oyster sauce* ‖ *1 tablespoon light soy sauce* ‖ *2 green onions, finely sliced* ‖ *½ cup dry-fried cashews (see page 19)* ‖ *ground white pepper*

ONE Remove the stems from the chilies; use scissors to cut each one into ½ inch pieces and discard the seeds. **TWO** Heat ½ tablespoon oil in a nonstick wok or skillet and stir-fry the chilies over medium heat for 1 minute. Remove from the wok. **THREE** Add 1 tablespoon oil and stir-fry the garlic for another 1–2 minutes or until lightly browned. **FOUR** Add the chicken and stock and stir-fry over high heat for 4–5 minutes or until the chicken is cooked. **FIVE** Add the red bell pepper, carrots, onions, oyster sauce, and soy sauce and stir-fry for 1–2 minutes. Add the green onions, chilies, and cashews. Spoon onto a serving plate, season with ground white pepper, and serve immediately.

Serves 4 with 2 other main dishes

NUTRIENT ANALYSIS PER SERVING 1334 kJ – 319 cal – 32 g protein – 8 g carbohydrate – 3 g sugars – 18 g fat – 4 g saturated fat – 1 g fiber – 330 mg sodium

HEALTHY TIP Cashews have a high vitamin C content, and they also contain iron, zinc, magnesium, selenium, and vitamin B1. They have antiseptic and cicatrizing properties and are considered good for toothaches and gums.

Panaeng chicken curry

Panaeng curry is a dry, rich, thick curry that is made with small amounts of coconut milk and a dry curry paste. This elegant dish is quick and easy to make and should have a mild taste.

INGREDIENTS *1½ tablespoons sunflower oil* ‖ *1 recipe Dry Curry Paste (see page 19) or 1–2 oz purchased dry curry paste* ‖ *1½ lb boneless, skinless chicken breasts, thinly sliced* ‖ *⅔ cup canned coconut milk, shaken well; reserve 2 tablespoons for garnish* ‖ *¼ cup Chicken Stock (see page 15) or water* ‖ *1 tablespoon fish sauce* ‖ *1 tablespoon palm or coconut sugar* ‖ *2 tablespoons Tamarind Purée (see page 22) or lemon juice*

TO SERVE *5 kaffir lime leaves, finely sliced* ‖ *1 long red chili, stemmed, seeded, and finely sliced*

ONE Heat the oil in a nonstick wok or skillet and stir-fry the dry curry paste over medium heat for 2 minutes or until fragrant. **TWO** Add the chicken and stir-fry for 5 minutes. **THREE** Add the coconut milk, stock, fish sauce, sugar, and tamarind purée or lemon juice and reduce heat to low. Simmer, uncovered, for about 5–7 minutes. This is meant to be a dry curry, but you can add a little more water during cooking if it dries out too much. Transfer the curry to a serving bowl, spoon the reserved warm coconut milk over the top, garnish with sliced kaffir lime leaves and chili, and serve immediately.

Serves 4 with 2 other main dishes

NUTRIENT ANALYSIS PER SERVING 1590 kJ – 380 cal – 44 g protein – 13 g carbohydrate – 9 g sugars – 17 g fat – 7 g saturated fat – 0 g fiber – 480 mg sodium

HEALTHY TIP A healthy option for cooking, sunflower oil is light in taste and appearance and supplies more vitamin E than any other vegetable oil.

Chicken liver with black peppercorns and garlic

The garlic and cilantro root impart an intense flavor, but there is also a lovely smooth texture from the chicken liver in this dish. You can use thinly sliced calves' liver as an alternative.

INGREDIENTS *1 lb chicken livers* ‖ *5 garlic cloves, roughly chopped* ‖ *10 cilantro roots, roughly chopped* ‖ *10 black peppercorns* ‖ *1½ tablespoons sunflower oil* ‖ *2 tablespoons Chicken Stock (see page 15), Vegetable Stock (see page 16), or water* ‖ *1 tablespoon oyster sauce* ‖ *1 tablespoon light soy sauce* ‖ *cilantro leaves, to garnish*

ONE Trim the chicken livers and slice them into bite-sized pieces. **TWO** Use a mortar and pestle or a blender to pound or blend the garlic and cilantro roots into a smooth paste. Add the peppercorns and continue to grind roughly. **THREE** Heat the oil in a nonstick wok or skillet and stir-fry the garlic paste over medium heat for 1–2 minutes or until fragrant. **FOUR** Add the liver, stock, oyster sauce, and soy sauce. Stir-fry for another 2–3 minutes or until the liver is light brown outside but a little pink and tender inside. Garnish with a few cilantro leaves and serve immediately.

Serves 4 with 3 other main dishes

NUTRIENT ANALYSIS PER SERVING 912 kJ – 218 cal – 25 g protein – 3 g carbohydrate – 0 g sugars – 12 g fat – 3 g saturated fat – 0 g fiber – 320 mg sodium

HEALTHY TIP Chicken liver is rich in vitamin A, which is good for the eyes, skin, and immune system. Other nutrients include trace elements, such as iron, selenium, and copper; the latter aids in the formation of blood cells and connective tissue.

Red curry chicken with Thai baby eggplants

This is a popular hot Thai curry made with a paste of dried red chilies and many fresh herbs. Using coconut milk cooked with chicken or whatever meat you prefer, you can create your own favorite red curry. Baby eggplants from Thailand vary in size. In this recipe, use eggplants that are about ½ inch across, or quarter larger ones.

INGREDIENTS *1½ tablespoons sunflower oil* ‖ *1 recipe Red Curry Paste (see page 18) or 1–2 oz purchased red curry paste* ‖ *14½ oz boneless, skinless chicken breasts, thinly sliced* ‖ *¾ cup canned coconut milk, shaken well* ‖ *¾ cup Chicken Stock (see page 15)* ‖ *7 oz Thai baby eggplants* ‖ *2 tablespoons fish sauce* ‖ *1½ tablespoons palm or coconut sugar* ‖ *5 kaffir lime leaves, torn in half*

TO SERVE *Thai sweet basil leaves*

ONE Heat the oil in a nonstick wok or skillet and stir-fry the red curry paste over medium heat for 2 minutes or until fragrant. **TWO** Add the chicken and stir-fry for 2–3 minutes. **THREE** Add the coconut milk, stock, Thai baby eggplants, fish sauce, sugar, and kaffir lime leaves and cook for another 5–7 minutes. Spoon into a serving bowl, garnish with Thai sweet basil leaves, and serve immediately.

Serves 4 with 2 other main dishes

NUTRIENT ANALYSIS PER SERVING 1373 kJ – 329 cal – 28 g protein – 14 g carbohydrate – 9 g sugars – 17 g fat – 7 g saturated fat – 2 g fiber – 740 mg sodium

HEALTHY TIP Thai baby eggplants have few calories and virtually no fat, and their meaty texture makes them a satisfying accompaniment to a delicious curry.

Yellow curry chicken with pineapple

Chicken and pineapple are a typically Thai combination; each goes well with yellow curry both in color and in flavor.

INGREDIENTS *1½ tablespoons sunflower oil* ‖ *1 recipe Yellow Curry Paste (see page 17)* ‖ *10 oz boneless, skinless chicken breasts, thinly sliced* ‖ *¾ cup canned coconut milk, shaken well* ‖ *¾ cup Chicken Stock (see page 15)* ‖ *10 oz pineapple, cut into 1 inch cubes* ‖ *1½ tablespoons fish sauce* ‖ *1 long red chili, stemmed, seeded, and finely sliced, to garnish*

ONE Heat the oil in a nonstick wok or skillet and stir-fry the yellow curry paste over medium heat for 2 minutes or until fragrant. **TWO** Add the chicken and stir-fry for 4–5 minutes. **THREE** Add the coconut milk, stock, pineapple, and fish sauce. Spoon into a serving bowl, garnish with chili, and serve immediately.

Serves 4 with 2 other main dishes

NUTRIENT ANALYSIS PER SERVING 1124 kJ – 269 cal – 19 g protein – 12 g carbohydrate – 9 g sugars – 16 g fat – 7 g saturated fat – 1 g fiber – 350 mg sodium

HEALTHY TIP Pineapple is high in the enzyme bromelain and the antioxidant vitamin C. Bromelain not only reduces the swelling, tenderness, and pain of bruising but also helps to relieve indigestion. Vitamin C helps to decrease the severity of colds and infections.

Stuffed omelet

A dish that is eaten occasionally rather than often, a stuffed omelet needs to be made neatly, with the sides folded over the meat like a package.

INGREDIENTS *1 tablespoon sunflower oil* ‖ *2 garlic cloves, finely chopped* ‖ *4 oz ground chicken or shrimp* ‖ *1 carrot, finely diced* ‖ *1 small onion, finely chopped* ‖ *½ cup green peas, thawed if frozen* ‖ *½ cup corn kernels, thawed if frozen* ‖ *½ red bell pepper, seeded and finely diced* ‖ *1 tablespoon fish sauce* ‖ *2 tablespoons tomato ketchup*

OMELET *3 large eggs* ‖ *1 tablespoon water* ‖ *ground white pepper* ‖ *2 tablespoons sunflower oil, divided*

TO SERVE *1 long red chili, seeded and shredded* ‖ *cilantro leaves*

ONE Heat the oil in a nonstick wok or skillet and stir-fry the garlic over medium heat until lightly browned. Add the chicken or shrimp and stir-fry for 3–4 minutes or until the meat is cooked. **TWO** Add the remaining ingredients and stir-fry for another 3–4 minutes. Keep this mixture warm while you cook the omelet. **THREE** Beat the eggs together with the water until slightly frothy; season with ground white pepper. **FOUR** Heat 1 tablespoon of oil in a nonstick pan and pour in half of the egg mixture. Swirl it around the pan so that it forms a thin omelet. When it has turned brown underneath and is almost set, gently flip it over to cook the top. **FIVE** Spoon half the filling into the center of the omelet and carefully fold it up so that the filling is completely enclosed and the omelet forms a neat square. Keep it warm while you make a second omelet in the same way. Serve both omelets on a serving plate, garnished with chili and a few cilantro leaves.

Serves 4 with 2 other main dishes

NUTRIENT ANALYSIS PER SERVING 447 kJ – 107 cal – 9 g protein – 9 g carbohydrate – 5 g sugars – 4 g fat – 1 g saturated fat – 2 g fiber – 360 mg sodium

HEALTHY TIP Eggs contain useful amounts of protein, which is essential for good health and well-being, plus vitamins A, B2, B12, and E.

Spicy ground duck

This tasty dish is served on a medley of fresh crispy vegetables, making it a good healthy choice. It can also be made with ground chicken or pork.

INGREDIENTS *10 oz ground lean duck* ‖ *3 tablespoons lemon juice* ‖ *1 tablespoon fish sauce* ‖ *1 lemongrass stalk (white part only), 5 inches long, finely sliced* ‖ *4 shallots, finely sliced* ‖ *5 kaffir lime leaves, finely sliced* ‖ *5 green onions, finely chopped* ‖ *1 tablespoon ground rice (see page 70)* ‖ *3–4 small red or green chilies, finely chopped or ½–1 teaspoon chili powder*

TO SERVE *mixed salad leaves* ‖ *mint leaves* ‖ *a selection of fresh vegetables, such as long green beans, tomatoes, and cabbage*

ONE Cook the duck, lemon juice, and fish sauce in a nonstick saucepan or wok over high heat. Use a spoon to crumble and break up the duck until the meat has separated and cooked through. Remove from heat. **TWO** Add the lemongrass, shallots, kaffir lime leaves, green onions, ground rice, and chilies to the duck and mix together. **THREE** Line a serving plate with a few mixed salad leaves, top with the duck mixture, garnish with mint leaves, and serve immediately with crispy vegetables.

Serves 4 with 3 other main dishes

NUTRIENT ANALYSIS PER SERVING 585 kJ – 139 cal – 17 g protein – 8 g carbohydrate – 2 g sugars – 4 g fat – 1 g saturated fat – 1 g fiber – 500 mg sodium

HEALTHY TIP Onions are rich in chromium, a trace mineral that improves glucose tolerance, lowers insulin levels, and decreases total cholesterol and triglyceride levels.

Red curry with duck and lychees

A luxurious but healthy dish, this is a curry you can enjoy with lychees, pineapple, or young coconut if you prefer.

INGREDIENTS *1 lb boneless duck breasts* ‖ *1 teaspoon sesame oil* ‖ *2 teaspoons light soy sauce* ‖ *½ inch fresh ginger root, peeled and finely chopped* ‖ *2 garlic cloves, finely chopped* ‖ *½ teaspoon ground allspice* ‖ *1½ tablespoons sunflower oil* ‖ *1 recipe Red Curry Paste (see page 18) or 1–2 oz purchased red curry paste* ‖ *¾ cup canned coconut milk, shaken well* ‖ *¾ cup Vegetable Stock (see page 16)* ‖ *2 tablespoons fish sauce* ‖ *1½ tablespoons palm or coconut sugar* ‖ *8 oz canned lychees, drained (discard the syrup)* ‖ *4 oz cherry tomatoes* ‖ *5 kaffir lime leaves, torn in half*

TO SERVE *Thai sweet basil leaves* ‖ *1 long red chili, stemmed, seeded, and finely sliced*

ONE Remove the skin and fat from the duck breasts and thinly slice the meat. Mix the meat with the sesame oil, soy sauce, ginger, garlic, and allspice and set aside to marinate for at least 30 minutes. **TWO** Heat the oil in a nonstick wok or skillet and stir-fry the red curry paste over medium heat for 2 minutes or until fragrant. **THREE** Add the meat, coconut milk, and stock and cook for 5–6 minutes or until the meat is cooked. Add the fish sauce, sugar, lychees, and tomatoes and cook for another 1–2 minutes, taking care not to let the tomatoes lose their shape. Add the kaffir lime leaves. Spoon into a serving bowl, garnish with a few Thai sweet basil leaves and chili slices and serve immediately.

Serves 4 with 2 other main dishes

NUTRIENT ANALYSIS PER SERVING 1600 kJ – 383 cal – 24 g protein – 29 g carbohydrate – 22 g sugars – 19 g fat – 8 g saturated fat – 2 g fiber – 780 mg sodium

HEALTHY TIP Duck is an excellent source of zinc and a good source of iron, providing three times as much iron as chicken. It has a similar protein content to chicken and turkey.

Steamed pork spare ribs with cilantro roots

Everyone in Thailand loves this fun-to-eat dish, and I have eaten it since I was a child. The ribs need to be chopped to short lengths to fit the steamer rack, and the dish is best if you can get baby back ribs. Ask your butcher to prepare them for you.

INGREDIENTS *2 lb pork spare ribs, chopped into 1½ inch lengths* ‖ *3 garlic cloves, finely chopped* ‖ *1 oz cilantro roots, cleaned and finely chopped* ‖ *½–1 inch fresh ginger root, peeled and finely chopped* ‖ *1 tablespoon light soy sauce* ‖ *1 tablespoon oyster sauce*

ONE Combine all ingredients in a large mixing bowl, using your fingers or a spoon to mix them. Cover with plastic wrap and let marinate for at least 3 hours or overnight in the refrigerator if time allows. **TWO** Fill a wok or steamer pan with water, place the bamboo steamer basket on a steamer rack, cover, and boil over high heat. **THREE** Place the marinated pork spare ribs on a plate. **FOUR** Taking care not to burn your hand, set the plate inside the steamer basket and simmer for 20 minutes or until all the spare ribs are cooked. Check and replenish the water every 10 minutes or so.

Serves 4 as a starter or 2 as a main course

NUTRIENT ANALYSIS PER SERVING 1020 kJ – 246 cal – 23 g protein – 2 g carbohydrate – 0 g sugars – 16 g fat – 6 g saturated fat – 0 g fiber – 330 mg sodium

HEALTHY TIP Cilantro is a member of the carrot family, but only Thai cuisine uses the roots as a flavoring. Cilantro has a calming effect on the stomach.

Pork with ginger

Children enjoy this dish, but only if the amount of ginger is reduced. Eaten with rice, it makes an excellent main dish.

INGREDIENTS *scant ¼ oz dried black fungus* ‖ *1½ tablespoons sunflower oil* ‖ *3–4 garlic cloves, finely chopped* ‖ *1 lb boneless pork tenderloins or boneless, skinless chicken breasts, thinly sliced* ‖ *1 small onion, cut into 8 pieces* ‖ *2 inches fresh ginger root, peeled and finely sliced* ‖ *1½ tablespoons oyster sauce* ‖ *¼ cup Vegetable Stock (see page 16) or water* ‖ *2 green onions, finely sliced*

TO SERVE *cilantro leaves* ‖ *ground white pepper*

ONE Soak the dried black fungus in hot water for 2–3 minutes or until soft, then drain. **TWO** Heat the oil in a nonstick wok or skillet and stir-fry the garlic over medium heat until lightly browned. **THREE** Add the pork or chicken and stir-fry for 4–5 minutes or until cooked through. **FOUR** Add the dried black fungus and the remaining ingredients and stir-fry for another 2–3 minutes. Spoon onto a serving plate, garnish with a few cilantro leaves, season with ground white pepper, and serve immediately.

Serves 4 with 2 other main dishes

NUTRIENT ANALYSIS PER SERVING 1000 kJ – 240 cal – 27 g protein – 4 g carbohydrate – 1 g sugars – 13 g fat – 4 g saturated fat – 0 g fiber – 325 mg sodium

HEALTHY TIP Ginger is a useful alternative remedy for travel sickness or morning sickness. In herbal medicine, it is used to aid digestion, to protect against respiratory and digestive infections, and to relieve gas or bloating.

Chinese okra with pork

Chinese okra, or turia, is a long, cucumber-shaped vegetable with ridges running along its length. It is available in many Asian stores.

INGREDIENTS *10 oz Chinese okra* ‖ *1½ tablespoons sunflower oil* ‖ *3 garlic cloves, finely chopped* ‖ *6 oz pork fillet, thinly sliced* ‖ *1 tablespoon Vegetable Stock (see page 16) or water* ‖ *1½ tablespoons oyster sauce* ‖ *ground white pepper*

ONE Use a knife to remove the skin of the okra and cut the flesh diagonally into slices that are 1 inch wide and 2 inches long. **TWO** Heat the oil in a nonstick wok or skillet and stir-fry the garlic over medium heat until lightly browned. **THREE** Add the pork and stir-fry for 2–3 minutes. **FOUR** Add the okra, stock, and oyster sauce and stir-fry for another 2–3 minutes or until the pork and okra are cooked. Season with ground white pepper and serve immediately.

Serves 4 with 2 other main dishes

NUTRIENT ANALYSIS PER SERVING 552 kJ – 132 cal – 12 g protein – 4 g carbohydrate – 2 g sugars – 8 g fat – 2 g saturated fat – 3 g fiber – 270 mg sodium

HEALTHY TIP Chinese okra is low in calories. A 3 oz serving contains just 20 calories but 20 percent of the recommended daily allowance of vitamin C.

Bamboo shoots with ground pork

The first time I tried this dish was just before I left Thailand to live in London. It is from the northeast of Thailand, has a lovely aroma, and is quite spicy from the red curry paste. You won't need a curry dish if you have this as a main course.

INGREDIENTS *1½ tablespoons sunflower oil* ‖ *½ recipe Red Curry Paste (see page 18) or 1½ tablespoons purchased red curry paste* ‖ *6 oz ground pork* ‖ *100 g canned bamboo shoots in water, drained* ‖ *1 tablespoon fish sauce*

ONE Heat the oil in a nonstick wok or skillet and stir-fry the red curry paste over medium heat for 2 minutes or until fragrant. **TWO** Add the ground pork and stir-fry until the meat has separated and cooked through. **THREE** Add the bamboo shoots and fish sauce and stir-fry for another 2–3 minutes.

Serves 4 with 2 other main dishes

NUTRIENT ANALYSIS PER SERVING 639 kJ – 154 cal – 13 g protein – 6 g carbohydrate – 2 g sugars – 8 g fat – 2 g saturated fat – 2 g fiber – 430 mg sodium

HEALTHY TIP Low in calories and fat, bamboo shoots are so high in fiber that a single serving can provide as much as one-tenth of the recommended daily amount. They are also a rich source of potassium, which helps maintain normal blood pressure and heart rate.

Green curry beef with bamboo shoots
Green curry is the classic Thai curry. It is more pungent than the other curries and should never be extremely hot.

INGREDIENTS *1½ tablespoons sunflower oil* ‖ *1 recipe Green Curry Paste (see page 18) or 1–2 oz purchased green curry paste* ‖ *14½ oz tender steak rump or fillet, thinly sliced* ‖ *¾ cup canned coconut milk, shaken well* ‖ *¾ cup Beef Stock (see page 15)* ‖ *5 oz canned bamboo shoots in water, drained* ‖ *2 tablespoons fish sauce* ‖ *1½ tablespoons palm or coconut sugar* ‖ *2 oz krachai, peeled and finely sliced (see page 10)* ‖ *5 kaffir lime leaves, torn in half*

TO SERVE *Thai sweet basil leaves* ‖ *1 long red chili, stemmed, seeded, and finely sliced*

ONE Heat the oil in a nonstick wok or skillet and stir-fry the green curry paste over medium heat for 2 minutes or until fragrant. **TWO** Add the beef and stir-fry for 2–3 minutes. **THREE** Add the coconut milk, stock, bamboo shoots, fish sauce, sugar, and krachai and cook for another 5–7 minutes. Add the kaffir lime leaves. Place in a serving bowl, garnish with Thai sweet basil leaves and the sliced chili, and serve immediately.

Serves 4 with 2 other main dishes

NUTRIENT ANALYSIS PER SERVING 1484 kJ – 356 cal – 28 g protein – 14 g carbohydrate – 8 g sugars – 21 g fat – 9 g saturated fat – 1 g fiber – 700 mg sodium

HEALTHY TIP According to nutritionists, lean beef can be part of a healthy diet when eaten in moderation. It is a good source of high-quality protein, iron, zinc, and B vitamins.

Beef with bell peppers

Bell peppers are used more widely in the West than in Eastern cuisine, but I hope you will agree that this dish is very much in the spirit of Thai food. The red and green bell peppers and dark, tender meat are an attractive combination.

INGREDIENTS *1½ tablespoons vegetable oil* ‖ *3 garlic cloves, finely chopped* ‖ *9 oz tender steak rump or fillet, thinly sliced* ‖ *3 tablespoons Thai Stock (see page 16), or Vegetable Stock (see page 16), or water* ‖ *4 oz red and green bell peppers, seeded and cut into bite-sized pieces* ‖ *1 onion, sliced* ‖ *1 tablespoon oyster sauce* ‖ *2 green onions, finely sliced* ‖ *ground white pepper*

ONE Heat the oil in a nonstick wok or skillet and stir-fry the garlic over medium heat until lightly browned. **TWO** Add the beef and stir-fry for 3–4 minutes. Add the stock, bell peppers, onion, and oyster sauce and stir-fry for another 2–3 minutes. Add the green onions and transfer to a serving plate. Season with ground white pepper and serve immediately.

Serves 4 with 2 other main dishes

NUTRIENT ANALYSIS PER SERVING 689 kJ – 165 cal – 16 g protein – 6 g carbohydrate – 4 g sugars – 9 g fat – 2 g saturated fat – 1 g fiber – 240 mg sodium

HEALTHY TIP Green bell peppers provide vitamin C and beta-carotene, both of which are believed to have strong protective antioxidant functions against cancer, heart disease, and stroke.

Massaman beef curry

This popular curry is typical of southern Thai cooking. Sweet flavors of mixed spices predominate, even though the curry is moderately hot. It is one of the very few dishes in Thai cooking that includes potatoes and roasted peanuts. If preferred, use lamb instead of beef.

INGREDIENTS *2 cinnamon sticks* ‖ *10 cardamom seeds* ‖ *4 star anise* ‖ *5 cloves* ‖ *1½ tablespoons sunflower oil* ‖ *1 recipe Massaman Curry Paste (see page 17) or 2 oz purchased massaman paste* ‖ *1½ lb beef flank or rump steak, cut into 2 inch cubes* ‖ *¾ cup canned coconut milk, shaken well* ‖ *1¾ cups Beef Stock (see page 15)* ‖ *2 onions, quartered* ‖ *2 tablespoons fish sauce* ‖ *2 tablespoons palm or coconut sugar* ‖ *3 tablespoons Tamarind Purée (see page 22) or lemon juice* ‖ *½ cup roasted peanuts (see page 19)* ‖ *8 oz potatoes, cut into 1 inch cubes* ‖ *1 long red chili, stemmed, seeded, and finely sliced, to garnish*

ONE Dry-fry the cinnamon stick, cardamom seeds, star anise, and cloves in a skillet or wok over low heat. Stir all the ingredients around for 2–3 minutes or until fragrant. Remove from pan. **TWO** Heat the oil in a nonstick wok or skillet and stir-fry the massaman paste over medium heat for 2 minutes or until fragrant. **THREE** Add the beef and cook for 2–3 minutes. Add the coconut milk, stock, onions, fish sauce, sugar, tamarind purée or lemon juice, dry-fried spices, and roasted peanuts. Gently simmer over medium heat for 20 minutes. **FOUR** Add the potatoes and continue to simmer, uncovered, over low heat for another 30 minutes. Transfer to a serving bowl, garnish with sliced chili, and serve immediately.

Serves 4 with 2 other main dishes

NUTRIENT ANALYSIS PER SERVING 2595 kJ – 620 cal – 48 g protein – 38 g carbohydrate – 19 g sugars – 31 g fat – 11 g saturated fat – 4 g fiber – 780 mg sodium

HEALTHY TIP Onions contain two compounds, allicin and sulforaphane, which are believed to reduce the risk of cancer. Some studies suggest that those compounds may also help to reduce blood cholesterol levels and reduce the risk of blood clot formation, thus helping to prevent coronary heart disease.

Stir-fried mixed vegetables

Firm stir-fried vegetables retain their nutritional value better than boiled vegetables. They complement all Thai meat and fish dishes and can even be a meal in themselves. Vegetarians should omit the oyster sauce and increase the amount of light soy sauce to 2 tablespoons.

INGREDIENTS *10 thin asparagus spears ‖ 10 baby corn ‖ 4 oz green beans ‖ 4 oz red and yellow bell peppers ‖ 4 oz small zucchini ‖ 4 oz snow peas, trimmed ‖ 1 small carrot or 4–5 baby carrots ‖ 1 tablespoon sesame seeds ‖ 4 oz small broccoli florets ‖ 4 oz bean sprouts ‖ 1 inch fresh ginger root, peeled and finely sliced ‖ 1½ tablespoons sunflower oil ‖ 2–3 garlic cloves, finely chopped ‖ ¼ cup Vegetable Stock (see page 16) or water ‖ 1 tablespoon light soy sauce ‖ 2 tablespoons oyster sauce ‖ cilantro leaves, to garnish*

ONE Prepare the vegetables. Cut off the tips of the asparagus and cut each stalk into 2 inch lengths. Cut the baby corn and green beans in half lengthwise at an angle. Halve and seed the bell peppers and cut the flesh into bite-sized pieces. Slice the zucchini thinly. Leave the snow peas whole, although if they are rather large cut them in half and trim. Peel and cut the carrot into matchsticks or scrub them if you are using whole baby carrots. **TWO** Dry-fry the sesame seeds in a small pan for 1–2 minutes or until lightly brown; set aside. **THREE** Blanch the asparagus stalks (not the tips), baby corn, green beans, zucchini, snow peas, carrots, and broccoli florets in boiling water for 30 seconds. Plunge into a bowl of ice water to ensure a crispy texture, drain, and transfer to a mixing bowl with the asparagus tips, bell peppers, bean sprouts, and ginger. **FOUR** Heat the oil in a nonstick wok or skillet and stir-fry the garlic over medium heat until lightly browned. Add the mixed vegetables and the remaining ingredients and stir-fry over high heat for 2–3 minutes. Transfer to a serving plate, garnish with a few cilantro leaves and toasted sesame seeds and serve immediately.

Serves 4 with 2 other main dishes

NUTRIENT ANALYSIS PER SERVING 790 kJ – 190 cal – 10 g protein – 19 g carbohydrate – 7 g sugars – 9 g fat – 1 g saturated fat – 6 g fiber – 430 mg sodium

HEALTHY TIP Asparagus and broccoli are excellent sources of folate, necessary for the production and maintenance of new cells. Broccoli also contains the phytochemical sulforaphane, which helps reduce the risk of cancer.

Stir-fried mixed vegetables with tofu

Thailand exports tons of baby corn to the West, so you can use some real Thai vegetables for this dish. Vegetarians should use 2½ tablespoons of light soy sauce and no oyster sauce.

INGREDIENTS *1 lb mixed vegetables, such as baby corn, thin asparagus spears, carrots, snow peas, and bean sprouts ‖ 1¼ lb firm tofu ‖ 1½ tablespoons sunflower oil ‖ 3 garlic cloves, finely chopped ‖ 1 inch fresh ginger root, peeled and finely sliced ‖ 2 tablespoons Vegetable Stock (see page 16) or water ‖ 1 tablespoon light soy sauce ‖ 1½ tablespoons oyster sauce ‖ cilantro leaves, to garnish*

ONE Prepare the vegetables. Cut the baby corn in half lengthwise. Cut off the tips of the asparagus and slice each stalk into 2 inch lengths. Cut the carrots into matchsticks. Trim the snow peas. **TWO** Blanch all the vegetables in boiling water for 30 seconds, plunge into a bowl of ice water to ensure a crispy texture, and drain. **THREE** Drain the tofu and cut into 1 inch cubes. **FOUR** Heat the oil in a nonstick wok or skillet and stir-fry the garlic over medium heat until lightly browned. **FIVE** Add the mixed vegetables, tofu, and remaining ingredients and gently stir-fry for 2–3 minutes, taking care not to let the tofu cubes lose their shape. Spoon into a serving bowl, garnish with a few cilantro leaves, and serve immediately.

Serves 4 with 2 other main dishes

NUTRIENT ANALYSIS PER SERVING 1217 kJ – 290 cal – 23 g protein – 22 g carbohydrate – 5 g sugars – 13 g fat – 2 g saturated fat – 8 g fiber – 330 mg sodium

HEALTHY TIP Asparagus is a rich source of many of the B vitamins, especially folate. New research suggests that folate may have a role in helping to protect against heart disease.

Jungle curry with mixed vegetables

This is a very hot curry that, unusually, does not use coconut milk. It can be made with any kind of meat or seafood. Vegetarians should omit the shrimp paste and fish sauce and use 2 tablespoons of light soy sauce.

INGREDIENTS *2 dried, long red chilies, each about 5 inches long* ‖ *1 lemongrass stalk (white part only), 3 inches long, finely sliced* ‖ *1 inch fresh galangal, peeled and finely sliced* ‖ *3 shallots, finely chopped* ‖ *2 garlic cloves, finely chopped* ‖ *1 tablespoon finely chopped krachai (see page 10)* ‖ *½ teaspoon shrimp paste* ‖ *12 oz mixed vegetables, such as baby corn, green beans, Thai baby eggplants, carrots, zucchini, and mixed mushrooms (oyster, shiitake, and button)* ‖ *2½ cups Vegetable Stock (see page 16)* ‖ *1 tablespoon fish sauce* ‖ *2–3 kaffir lime leaves, torn, to garnish*

ONE Remove the stems and slit the chilies lengthwise with a sharp knife; discard all the seeds and roughly chop the flesh. Soak the chilies in hot water for 2 minutes or until soft, then drain. **TWO** Use a mortar and pestle to grind and pound the chilies, lemongrass, and galangal into a paste. **THREE** Add the shallots, garlic, krachai, and shrimp paste and continue to pound into a smooth paste. **FOUR** Prepare the vegetables. Cut the baby corn and green beans in half lengthwise at an angle. Slice the carrots and zucchini diagonally. Cut the mushrooms in half if they are large and remove and discard any hard stalks. **FIVE** Put the stock, chili paste, and fish sauce in a large saucepan and bring it to a boil. Add all the mixed vegetables and cook for another 4–5 minutes. Garnish with the kaffir lime leaves and serve immediately.

Serves 4 with 2 main dishes

NUTRIENT ANALYSIS PER SERVING 140 kJ – 33 cal – 2 g protein – 5 g carbohydrate – 2 g sugars – 1 g fat – 0 g saturated fat – 3 g fiber – 210 mg sodium

HEALTHY TIP Green beans are a good source of vitamin B folate, which is essential for a healthy pregnancy. Doctors say it is important to ensure a good intake of folate in the early stages of pregnancy to prevent spina bifida. Folate may also have a role in helping to protect against heart disease.

Stir-fried mushrooms with ginger

There are so many health benefits from eating mushrooms that I have included another delicious combination using fresh ginger. It's just a side dish, but everyone will enjoy it. Vegetarians can use light soy sauce instead of the oyster sauce.

INGREDIENTS *scant ¼ oz dried black fungus* ‖ *1½ tablespoons sunflower oil* ‖ *3 garlic cloves, finely chopped* ‖ *1 lb mixed mushrooms, such as oyster, shiitake, and button* ‖ *1 small onion, cut into 6 wedges* ‖ *3 tablespoons Vegetable Stock (see page 16) or water* ‖ *2 tablespoons oyster sauce* ‖ *2 inches fresh ginger root, peeled and finely sliced* ‖ *2 green onions, sliced diagonally* ‖ *cilantro leaves, to garnish*

ONE Soak the dried black fungus in hot water for 2–3 minutes or until soft, then drain. Remove and discard the hard stalks. **TWO** Heat the oil in a nonstick wok or skillet and stir-fry the garlic over medium heat until lightly browned. **THREE** Cut any large mushrooms in half; remove and discard any hard stalks. Add the black fungus, mushrooms, and remaining ingredients to the wok and stir-fry over high heat for 4–5 minutes. Transfer to a serving plate, garnish with a few cilantro leaves, and serve immediately.

Serves 4 with 2 main dishes

NUTRIENT ANALYSIS PER SERVING 356 kJ – 86 cal – 3 g protein – 5 g carbohydrate – 1 g sugars – 6 g fat – 1 g saturated fat – 3 g fiber – 425 mg sodium

HEALTHY TIP Mushrooms provide protein, fiber, B vitamins, and vitamin C, as well as calcium and other minerals. Medicinal mushrooms, such as shiitake, have been shown to boost heart health, ward off viruses, and combat allergies, among other benefits.

Tomato and green onion omelet

This is a quick dish, easy to prepare and cook. It works best with cherry tomatoes and is served with chili and lime juice to add a touch of heat and freshness. Serve with Chili and Lime Sauce *(see page 21)*.

INGREDIENTS *4 large eggs* ‖ *1 tablespoon light soy sauce* ‖ *ground white pepper, to taste* ‖ *4 green onions, finely sliced* ‖ *8 cherry tomatoes, cut in half* ‖ *1½ tablespoons sunflower oil* ‖ *cilantro leaves, to garnish*

ONE In a bowl, beat together the eggs, soy sauce, and ground white pepper, whisking until slightly frothy. Add the green onions and tomatoes. **TWO** Heat the oil in a nonstick wok or skillet and add the egg mixture. Cook for 1–2 minutes or until lightly browned, then flip the omelet to brown the other side. Transfer to a serving plate and garnish with a few cilantro leaves.

Serves 4

NUTRIENT ANALYSIS PER SERVING 583 kJ – 140 cal – 8 g protein – 2 g carbohydrate – 1 g sugars – 12 g fat – 2 g saturated fat – 0 g fiber – 80 mg sodium

HEALTHY TIP Tomatoes contain lycopene, a carotenoid compound that acts as an antioxidant. Recent studies suggest that lycopene may help to protect against bladder and pancreatic cancers.

Pan-fried tofu with three-flavor sauce

Three-flavor sauce combines three opposing flavors—sweet, sour, and spicy—and it is the perfect accompaniment to pan-fried tofu. Vegetarians can use light soy sauce instead of fish sauce.

INGREDIENTS *2 garlic cloves, roughly chopped* ‖ *3 shallots, roughly chopped* ‖ *5 long red chilies, seeded and roughly chopped* ‖ *3 cilantro roots, roughly chopped* ‖ *sunflower oil, for frying* ‖ *2 tablespoons Vegetable Stock (see page 16) or water* ‖ *2 tablespoons Tamarind Purée (see page 22) or lemon juice* ‖ *1 tablespoon fish sauce* ‖ *1 tablespoon palm or coconut sugar* ‖ *1 lb firm tofu, drained and cut into 1 inch cubes* ‖ *3–4 tablespoons all-purpose flour* ‖ *pinch of ground white pepper* ‖ *Thai sweet basil leaves, to garnish*

ONE Use a mortar and pestle to pound the garlic, shallots, chilies, and cilantro roots into a rough paste. **TWO** Heat 1 tablespoon oil in a nonstick wok or skillet and stir-fry the chili paste over medium heat for 2 minutes or until fragrant. Add the stock, tamarind purée or lemon juice, fish sauce, and sugar and cook for another minute until the sugar has dissolved. Keep warm. **THREE** Pat the tofu cubes dry with paper towels. Mix the flour and ground white pepper together on a plate and gently press the tofu cubes into the mixture so that they are evenly coated. **FOUR** Heat a little sunflower oil in a nonstick skillet and gently fry the tofu cubes in batches, making sure there is a slight gap between each piece. Fry for 1 minute on each side or until lightly browned. Add a little more oil to the pan before cooking each batch. Pour the warm chili sauce over the tofu, garnish with a few Thai sweet basil leaves, and serve immediately.

Serves 4 with 2 other main dishes

NUTRIENT ANALYSIS PER SERVING 1067 kJ – 255 cal – 13 g protein – 22 g carbohydrate – 7 g sugars – 13 g fat – 2 g saturated fat – 1 g fiber – 220 mg sodium

HEALTHY TIP U.S. and Mexican researchers have identified an antibacterial compound in cilantro called dodecenal, a potent antibiotic capable of fighting salmonella.

Bitter melon omelet

Shaped like a fat cucumber, bitter melon has a shiny, bumpy skin with ridges running lengthwise. It is an acquired taste, but one worth trying if you enjoy other Thai dishes.

INGREDIENTS *6 oz bitter melon* ‖ *½ teaspoon salt* ‖ *4 large eggs* ‖ *1 tablespoon light soy sauce* ‖ *1½ tablespoons sunflower oil* ‖ *3 garlic cloves, finely chopped* ‖ *ground white pepper*

ONE Clean and cut the bitter melon into 1 inch rings, discarding all the seeds. Cut each ring in half and cut out the hard inner sleeve, which is about ⅛ inch thick. Finely slice the bitter melon pieces, put them in a bowl, sprinkle with salt, and stir. Let stand for 30 minutes so that the salt draws the bitter taste out of the melon. Rinse the bitter melon in water to remove the salt; drain. **TWO** In a bowl, beat the eggs with the soy sauce until slightly frothy. **THREE** Heat the oil in a nonstick wok or skillet and stir-fry the garlic over medium heat until lightly browned. Add the bitter melon and stir-fry for 2–3 minutes. **FOUR** Pour the egg mixture over the bitter melon and cook for 1–2 minutes or until lightly browned, then flip the omelet over to brown the other side. Transfer to a serving plate, season with ground white pepper, and serve with Sesame Oil Sauce *(see page 21).*

Serves 4

NUTRIENT ANALYSIS PER SERVING 530 kJ – 128 cal – 8 g protein – 1 g carbohydrate – 1 g sugars – 10 g fat – 2 g saturated fat – 0 g fiber – 320 mg sodium

HEALTHY TIP Bitter melon has twice as much beta-carotene as broccoli, twice the calcium of spinach, and twice the potassium of bananas. It is rich in iron and contains vitamins C and B1, B2, and B3. It also contains an insulin-like compound that reduces blood sugar and is a source of phosphorus and dietary fiber.

Vegetable curry

There are so many curried meat dishes that it is easy to forget that vegetarians can enjoy curry, too. This one, with sugarsnap peas and other vegetables, is really delicious. Vegetarians should use Vegetable Stock *(see page 16)* instead of chicken stock and light soy sauce instead of fish sauce.

INGREDIENTS *1½ tablespoons vegetable oil ‖ 1 recipe Dry Curry Paste (see page 19) or 1–2 oz purchased dry curry paste ‖ ⅔ cup canned coconut milk, shaken well ‖ ¼ cup Chicken Stock (see page 15) or water ‖ 7 oz sugarsnap or snow peas, trimmed ‖ 2 medium carrots, cut into matchsticks ‖ 4 oz baby corn, cut in half lengthwise ‖ 1 cup fresh, bite-sized pineapple pieces ‖ 5 oz cherry tomatoes ‖ 2 tablespoons Tamarind Purée (see page 22) or lemon juice ‖ 1 tablespoon fish sauce ‖ 1 tablespoon palm or coconut sugar ‖ 2 kaffir lime leaves ‖ 1 long red chili, stemmed, seeded, and finely sliced, to garnish*

ONE Heat the oil in a nonstick wok or skillet and stir-fry the dry curry paste over medium heat for 2 minutes or until fragrant. **TWO** Add the coconut milk and stock and heat just to boiling. Add the peas, carrots, and baby corn and cook for 3–4 minutes. **THREE** Add the pineapple, tomatoes, tamarind purée or lemon juice, fish sauce, sugar, and kaffir lime leaves. Simmer uncovered for another 2–3 minutes. Spoon the curry into a serving bowl, garnish with the chili, and serve immediately.

Serves 4 with 3 main dishes

NUTRIENT ANALYSIS PER SERVING 892 kJ – 218 cal – 6 g protein – 22 g carbohydrate – 16 g sugars – 12 g fat – 5 g saturated fat – 2 g fiber – 720 mg sodium

HEALTHY TIP Sugarsnap peas provide a good amount of soluble fiber, which can help lower high blood cholesterol levels. They are also a good source of vitamin C.

Chinese cabbage with tofu

Chinese cabbage is a loose-leaf cabbage with an elongated, narrow shape and crinkly leaves. The leaves are pale green at the top and white at the bottom. You could use Romaine lettuce if you can't find Chinese cabbage. Vegetarians should omit the oyster sauce and use 1½ tablespoons light soy sauce.

INGREDIENTS 6 oz Chinese cabbage ‖ 1½ tablespoons sunflower oil ‖ 2–3 garlic cloves, finely chopped ‖ 1 celery stick, cut into ½ inch pieces ‖ ½ red bell pepper, seeded and cut into bite-sized pieces ‖ 12 oz firm tofu, cut into ½ inch cubes ‖ 1 tablespoon light soy sauce ‖ 1 tablespoon oyster sauce ‖ 1 red chili, about 5 inches long, stemmed, seeded, and finely sliced ‖ 2 green onions, finely sliced ‖ cilantro leaves, to garnish

ONE Trim and cut the white stalks of the Chinese cabbage into 2 inch lengths. Tear or coarsely shred the green leaves into manageable pieces. **TWO** Heat the oil in a nonstick wok or skillet and stir-fry the garlic over medium heat until lightly browned. **THREE** Add the white stalks of the Chinese cabbage, the celery, and red bell pepper and stir-fry for 2 minutes. Add the tofu and the green cabbage leaves and stir-fry for another 2–3 minutes or until the leaves start to wilt. Add the remaining ingredients and stir-fry for a few more minutes. Transfer to a serving plate, garnish with a few cilantro leaves, and serve immediately.

Serves 4 with 2 other main dishes

NUTRIENT ANALYSIS PER SERVING 539 kJ – 130 cal – 9 g protein – 4 g carbohydrate – 2 g sugars – 8 g fat – 1 g saturated fat – 1 g fiber – 220 mg sodium

HEALTHY TIP Celery contains pthalides, which are helpful in regulating blood pressure by relaxing the muscles of the arteries. High in vitamin C, celery also provides potassium and folacin.

Mixed vegetables with sweet and sour sauce

Few dishes are as healthy as mixed vegetables, especially when they are lightly stir-fried rather than boiled. Vegetarians should replace the fish sauce with 1 tablespoon of light soy sauce.

INGREDIENTS *1 lb mixed vegetables, such as baby corn, green beans, carrots, zucchini, and red and yellow bell peppers* ‖ *1 onion* ‖ *2 tomatoes* ‖ *8 oz canned pineapple slices in light syrup* ‖ *2 tablespoons Vegetable Stock (see page 16) or water* ‖ *½ tablespoon cornstarch* ‖ *1½ tablespoons tomato ketchup* ‖ *½ tablespoon fish sauce* ‖ *1½ tablespoons sunflower oil* ‖ *3 garlic cloves, finely chopped* ‖ *boiled rice, to serve*

ONE Prepare the vegetables. Cut the baby corn and green beans in half lengthwise at an angle. Cut the carrots into matchsticks. Cut the unpeeled zucchini in half lengthwise and then into thick slices. Core and seed the bell peppers and cut the flesh into bite-sized pieces. Cut the onion into 8 slices and the tomatoes into quarters. **TWO** Drain the pineapple (reserving the syrup) and cut each slice into 4 pieces. Mix the syrup (about 6 tablespoons) with the stock, cornstarch, ketchup, and fish sauce in a small bowl to make a smooth paste. **THREE** Heat the oil in a nonstick wok or skillet and stir-fry the garlic over medium heat until it is lightly browned. Add the corn, beans, carrots, zucchini, red and yellow bell peppers, and onion and stir-fry for 4–5 minutes. **FOUR** Add the pineapple pieces, tomato, and pineapple syrup mixture and stir together for another minute. Transfer to a serving dish and serve immediately with boiled rice.

Serves 4

NUTRIENT ANALYSIS PER SERVING 590 kJ – 140 cal – 3 g protein – 23 g carbohydrate – 18 g sugars – 5 g fat – 1 g saturated fat – 3 g fiber – 345 mg sodium

HEALTHY TIP Red bell peppers are an excellent source of vitamin C and are rich in beta-carotene. Both of those nutrients are powerful antioxidants, which can help combat the damaging effects of free radicals and protect against many diseases, including cancer and heart disease.

Rice and noodles

Rice soup with ground pork

As an alternative to pork, you can use chicken or shrimp if you prefer. Spinach can be substituted for Chinese cabbage if it is difficult to find.

INGREDIENTS *3 cilantro roots, roughly chopped* ‖ *3 garlic cloves, roughly chopped* ‖ *¼ teaspoon ground white pepper* ‖ *13 oz ground pork* ‖ *7½ cups Vegetable Stock (see page 16)* ‖ *3 tablespoons light soy sauce* ‖ *1 tablespoon preserved radish, finely chopped (optional)* ‖ *1 recipe Boiled Jasmine Rice (see page 22)* ‖ *1 inch fresh ginger root, peeled and finely sliced* ‖ *2 oz Chinese cabbage leaves, roughly chopped*

TO SERVE *2 green onions, finely chopped* ‖ *cilantro leaves* ‖ *ground white pepper*

ONE Use a mortar and pestle to grind the cilantro roots, garlic, and ground white pepper into a paste. **TWO** Transfer the cilantro paste to a bowl and combine with the pork. **THREE** Put the stock in a saucepan and heat just to boiling. Add the soy sauce, preserved radish (if using), and rice. **FOUR** Using a spoon or your wet fingers, shape the ground meat into small balls about ½ inch across and lower into the rice soup. Cook over medium heat for 3 minutes. **FIVE** Add the ginger and Chinese cabbage. Cook for another 1–2 minutes. Spoon into a serving bowl, garnish with green onions and a few cilantro leaves, season with ground white pepper, and serve immediately.

Serves 4 as a main dish

NUTRIENT ANALYSIS PER SERVING 1487 kJ – 353 cal – 25 g protein – 48 g carbohydrate – 0 g sugars – 8 g fat – 3 g saturated fat– 1 g fiber – 85 mg sodium

HEALTHY TIP Although pork today is leaner than ever before, it will be even healthier if you remove any visible fat. Pork contains high levels of vitamins B12, B6, thiamin, niacin, and riboflavin and is also rich in phosphorus, zinc, potassium, iron, and magnesium.

Rice soup with seafood and mushrooms To eat in Thailand

is to eat rice, so it will come as no surprise to find rice in desserts, or, as here, in soups.

INGREDIENTS *10 oz mixed seafood, such as white fish fillet, shrimp, scallops, and squid* ‖ *2 oz mixed mushrooms, such as oyster, chestnut, and shiitake* ‖ *7½ cups Vegetable Stock (see page 16)* ‖ *4 tablespoons light soy sauce* ‖ *1 tablespoon preserved radish, finely chopped (optional)* ‖ *1 recipe Boiled Jasmine Rice (see page 22)* ‖ *1 inch fresh ginger root, peeled and finely sliced*

TO SERVE *2 green onions, finely sliced diagonally* ‖ *cilantro leaves* ‖ *ground white pepper*

ONE Prepare the mixed seafood *(see page 12)*. Cut any large mushrooms in half and remove the hard stalks. **TWO** Put the stock in a saucepan and heat just to boiling. Add the soy sauce, preserved radish (if using), and rice and cook over medium heat for 2–3 minutes. **THREE** Add the mixed seafood, mushrooms, and ginger. Cook for another 2–3 minutes. Spoon into a serving bowl, garnish with green onions and a few cilantro leaves, season with ground white pepper, and serve immediately.

Serves 4 as a main dish

NUTRIENT ANALYSIS PER SERVING 1157 kJ – 273 cal – 19 g protein – 49 g carbohydrate – 0 g sugars – 1 g fat – 0 g saturated fat – 5 g fiber – 110 mg sodium

HEALTHY TIP Widely available in supermarkets everywhere in the West, shiitake mushrooms have been used medicinally by the Chinese for more than 6,000 years. They strengthen the immune system and reduce cholesterol levels.

Rice noodles with seafood

This noodle dish uses large white noodles and is one of the best known of its type. It is served at all times of the day or night in Thailand. Its light, bitter taste comes from Chinese kale.

INGREDIENTS *12 oz dried white rice noodles, ½ inch wide* ‖ *2 cups Seafood Stock (see page 16)* ‖ *1 tablespoon oyster sauce* ‖ *2 tablespoons light soy sauce* ‖ *1 tablespoon black or yellow bean sauce (optional) (see page 10)* ‖ *2 tablespoons cornstarch* ‖ *2½ tablespoons sunflower oil, divided* ‖ *5–6 garlic cloves, finely chopped* ‖ *12 oz Chinese kale, cut into 1 inch pieces, top leaves separated* ‖ *1 lb mixed seafood, such as raw, large- or medium-sized shrimp, white fish fillet (sea bass or cod), scallops, and squid* ‖ *ground white pepper*

ONE Soak the noodles in a bowl of water for 4–5 hours or, preferably, overnight. Drain. **TWO** Mix the stock, oyster sauce, soy sauce, black or yellow bean sauce (if using), and cornstarch in a bowl. **THREE** Heat 1 tablespoon oil in a nonstick wok or saucepan and stir-fry the noodles for 4–5 minutes or until cooked. Set aside and keep warm. **FOUR** Heat the remaining oil in the same wok and stir-fry the garlic over medium heat until lightly browned. Add the stalks of the Chinese kale and the mixed seafood and stir-fry for 2–3 minutes. **FIVE** Add the sauce mixture and top leaves of the kale and mix together for another minute or so. Spoon the mixed seafood and Chinese kale over the warm noodles, season with ground white pepper, and serve immediately.

Serves 4 as a main dish

NUTRIENT ANALYSIS PER SERVING 2382 kJ – 569 cal – 27 g protein – 90 g carbohydrate – 2 g sugars – 10 g fat – 1 g saturated fat – 3 g fiber – 790 mg sodium

HEALTHY TIP Chinese kale contains a lot of sulfur, and its juice is sometimes used for treating stomach and duodenal ulcers. It is an exceptional source of chlorophyll, calcium, iron, and vitamin A.

Thai-fried noodles with shrimp

If you are cooking this dish in an average-sized wok or skillet, it will be easier to make it for two people at a time, using half the ingredients and then repeating. It is one of the most famous noodle dishes in Thailand.

INGREDIENTS *1 lb large- or medium-sized raw shrimp, shelled and deveined* ‖ *10 oz dried sen lek noodles* ‖ *4 tablespoons Tamarind Purée (see page 22) or lemon juice* ‖ *2½ tablespoons fish sauce* ‖ *3 tablespoons tomato ketchup* ‖ *3 tablespoons sunflower oil, divided* ‖ *5 garlic cloves, finely chopped* ‖ *4 eggs* ‖ *2 carrots, shredded* ‖ *½ teaspoon chili powder (or to taste)* ‖ *2 tablespoons ground dried shrimp* ‖ *2 tablespoons preserved turnip, finely chopped (optional)* ‖ *5–6 tablespoons chopped roasted peanuts (see page 19)* ‖ *12 oz bean sprouts* ‖ *4 green onions, finely sliced*

TO SERVE *1 long red chili, seeded and shredded* ‖ *cilantro leaves* ‖ *lemon wedges*

ONE Prepare the shrimp *(see page 12)*. Soak the noodles in water for 4–5 hours or overnight if time allows. Drain. **TWO** Combine the tamarind purée or lemon juice, fish sauce, and tomato ketchup in a bowl and set aside. **THREE** Heat 1½ tablespoons of the oil in a nonstick wok or skillet and stir-fry the garlic over medium heat until lightly browned. Add the shrimp and cook for 1–2 minutes, then move the shrimp to the sides of the wok. Add the remaining oil to the wok. Add the eggs and stir to scramble for 1–2 minutes. Add the noodles and carrots and stir-fry together for another 2 minutes. Add the tamarind purée or lemon juice mixture, chili powder, ground dried shrimp, preserved turnip (if using), and half the roasted peanuts. Add half the bean sprouts and all the green onions. Spoon onto a serving plate and top with the remaining peanuts. Garnish with chilies and cilantro leaves, arrange the lemon wedges and remaining bean sprouts at the side of the dish, and serve immediately.

Serves 4 as a main dish

NUTRIENT ANALYSIS PER SERVING 3111 kJ – 746 cal – 45 g protein – 80 g carbohydrate – 8 g sugars – 26 g fat – 5 g saturated fat – 2 g fiber – 1260 mg sodium

HEALTHY TIP *Sen lek* noodles are narrow, ¼ inch (5 mm) wide rice noodles and are considered to be healthier than pasta, which is made from eggs and flour.

Fried rice with shrimp, crab, and curry powder

This looks like a grand "restaurant" dish, but it is one that can easily be cooked at home if you have a reliable fishmonger. If you are using an average-sized wok, it will be easier to use half the ingredients at a time and to repeat the process. Keep in mind that canned crab is salty, so do not automatically add extra salt until you have tasted the dish.

INGREDIENTS *8 oz shrimp, shelled and deveined* ‖ *3 tablespoons sunflower oil* ‖ *5–6 garlic cloves, finely chopped* ‖ *4 eggs* ‖ *6 cups cooked rice, chilled in the refrigerator overnight* ‖ *8 oz canned crab meat, drained* ‖ *2 teaspoons curry powder* ‖ *1½ tablespoons light soy sauce* ‖ *1 onion, sliced* ‖ *2 green onions, finely sliced* ‖ *about 8 cooked crab claws, 4 oz total*

TO SERVE *½ long red or green chili, stemmed, seeded, and finely sliced* ‖ *cilantro leaves*

ONE Prepare the shrimp *(see page 12)*. **TWO** Heat the oil in a nonstick wok or skillet and stir-fry the garlic over medium heat until lightly browned. **THREE** Add the shrimp and stir-fry over high heat for 1–2 minutes. Use a spatula to move the shrimp to the sides of the wok. **FOUR** Add the eggs and stir to scramble for 1–2 minutes. **FIVE** Add the rice, crab meat, curry powder, soy sauce, and onion and cook, stirring, for 1–2 minutes. Add the green onions. In the last minutes of cooking add the crab claws. Transfer to a serving dish, garnish with the chili and a few cilantro leaves, and serve immediately.

Serves 4 as main dish

NUTRIENT ANALYSIS PER SERVING 2517 kJ – 598 cal – 37 g protein – 79 g carbohydrate – 2 g sugars – 16 g fat – 3 g saturated fat – 6 g fiber – 570 mg sodium

HEALTHY TIP Crab is an excellent source of selenium and a good source of magnesium, vitamin B6, and folate.

Fried rice with pineapple

This is an easy way to enjoy fried rice with pineapple, which is a classic but sometimes complicated restaurant dish. You will find it easier to halve the ingredients and make enough for two people at a time, and then repeat the process.

INGREDIENTS *3 tablespoons sunflower oil* ‖ *5 garlic cloves, finely chopped* ‖ *10 oz raw shrimp* ‖ *10 oz ham, thinly sliced* ‖ *½ cup corn kernels, thawed if frozen* ‖ *½ cup green peas, thawed if frozen* ‖ *1 red bell pepper, seeded and finely sliced* ‖ *1 inch fresh ginger root, peeled and finely sliced* ‖ *1 recipe Boiled Jasmine Rice (see page 22), chilled in the refrigerator overnight* ‖ *2 tablespoons light soy sauce* ‖ *10 oz pineapple, cut into small cubes* ‖ *⅓ cup dry-fried cashews*

TO SERVE *1 large red chili, seeded and finely shredded* ‖ *cilantro leaves*

ONE Heat the oil in a nonstick wok or skillet and stir-fry the garlic over medium heat until lightly browned. **TWO** Add the shrimp, ham, corn, peas, red bell pepper, and ginger and stir-fry for 2 minutes or until the shrimp open and turn pink. **THREE** Add the boiled rice, soy sauce, and pineapple, mix together and cook over medium heat for 4–5 minutes. Spoon the fried rice onto a serving dish, garnish with the chili and a few cilantro leaves, and serve immediately.

Serves 4 as a main dish

NUTRIENT ANALYSIS PER SERVING 2892 kJ – 600 cal – 39 g protein – 90 g carbohydrate – 11 g sugars – 20 g fat – 4 g saturated fat – 6 g fiber – 940 mg sodium

HEALTHY TIP Pineapple is high in the enzyme bromelain and the antioxidant vitamin C. Bromelain is a natural anti-inflammatory agent that helps relieve the symptoms of rheumatoid arthritis while also breaking down the amino acid bonds in proteins, thus promoting good digestion.

Fresh egg noodles with mixed vegetables

Use fresh egg noodles if they are available, but you can also use dried egg noodles from a package and soak them overnight in water at room temperature. If you have a medium-sized wok, you will find it easier to cook half the ingredients at a time and then repeat the process.

INGREDIENTS *2 tablespoons sunflower oil* ‖ *5–6 garlic cloves, finely chopped* ‖ *16 oz egg noodles* ‖ *1 lb mixed vegetables, such as snow peas, yellow or red bell peppers, small broccoli florets, baby corn, and baby carrots,* ‖ *2 tablespoons Vegetable Stock (see page 16) or water* ‖ *1½ tablespoons oyster sauce* ‖ *1 tablespoon light soy sauce* ‖ *4 oz bean sprouts* ‖ *3 green onions, finely sliced* ‖ *cilantro leaves, to garnish*

ONE Heat the oil in a nonstick wok or skillet and stir-fry the garlic over medium heat until lightly browned. **TWO** Add the noodles and stir-fry over high heat for 1–2 minutes. **THREE** Trim the snow peas. Seed the peppers and cut the flesh into bite-sized pieces. Add the mixed vegetables, stock, oyster sauce, and soy sauce and stir-fry for 3–4 minutes. Add the bean sprouts and green onions and stir-fry for another minute or so. Transfer to a serving dish, garnish with a few cilantro leaves, and serve immediately.

Serves 4 as a main dish

NUTRIENT ANALYSIS PER SERVING 2537 kJ – 600 cal – 20 g protein – 99 g carbohydrate – 8 g sugars – 16 g fat – 4 g saturated fat – 8 g fiber – 835 mg sodium

HEALTHY TIP Egg noodles, containing up to 20 percent whole eggs, are an excellent source of selenium, thiamine, and folate and are a good source of niacin.

Fried rice with seafood

Fried rice dishes always use rice that has been cooked, such as rice left over from a previous meal. A lovely mixture of seafood with fried rice makes a typical seaside dish, available all along the coasts of Thailand. If you are using a medium-sized wok, use half the ingredients at a time and repeat the process.

INGREDIENTS *1 lb mixed seafood, such as raw shrimp, scallops, squid, and white fish fillet (cod or halibut)* ‖ *3 tablespoons sunflower oil* ‖ *4 garlic cloves, finely chopped* ‖ *6 cups cooked rice, chilled in the refrigerator overnight* ‖ *2 onions, sliced* ‖ *1 inch fresh ginger root, peeled and finely sliced* ‖ *2½ tablespoons light soy sauce* ‖ *3 green onions, finely sliced* ‖ *1 long red or green chili, stemmed, seeded, and finely sliced, to garnish*

ONE Prepare the mixed seafood *(see page 12)*. **TWO** Heat the oil in a nonstick wok or skillet and stir-fry the garlic over medium heat until lightly browned. **THREE** Add the mixed seafood mixture and stir-fry over high heat for 1–2 minutes. Add the cooked rice, onions, ginger, and soy sauce and stir-fry for 3–4 minutes. Add the green onions. Transfer to a serving plate, garnish with the chili, and serve immediately.

Serves 4 as main dish

NUTRIENT ANALYSIS PER SERVING 2235 kJ – 530 cal – 30 g protein – 83 g carbohydrate – 5 g sugars – 10 g fat – 1 g saturated fat – 5 g fiber – 180 mg sodium

HEALTHY TIP All doctors recommend that we eat seafood regularly. It is a lean source of protein with plenty of omega-3 fatty acids, which help prevent heart disease, eczema, arthritis, inflammation, auto-immune disease, hypertension, cancer, and even depression.

Desserts

Watermelon sorbet

Thais know how to keep cool in hot weather, and there is no better way than eating this delightfully refreshing dessert.

INGREDIENTS *flesh of small sweet red watermelon, about 5 cups, seeded* ‖ *juice of 1 orange* ‖ *rind of ½ orange* ‖ *½ inch fresh root ginger, peeled and finely sliced*

ONE Chop the watermelon into cubes and place in the bowl of a food processor with the orange juice, orange rind, and ginger. Process for 1–2 minutes or until smooth. **TWO** Pour the mixture into a freezer box or other container and freeze for 1½ hours or until half-frozen. Take the mixture out of the freezer and blend again in a food processor. Return to the container. Whisk at least twice more during the freezing time. There should be plenty of air whipped into the sorbet or it will be too icy and hard. Cover and freeze completely.

Serves 4–6

NUTRIENT ANALYSIS PER SERVING 540 kJ – 126 cal – 2 g protein – 29 g carbohydrate – 1 g sugars – 1 g fat – 0 g saturated fat – 1 g fiber – trace sodium

HEALTHY TIP Watermelon is packed with some of the most important antioxidants in nature. It is an excellent source of vitamin C, a very good source of vitamin B6, and it also provides vitamin B1, magnesium, and potassium. A slice of watermelon weighing 7 oz contains just 42 calories.

Lemongrass and lime sorbet
Nothing could be fresher and more enjoyable on a summer's day than a cooling bowl of lemongrass and lime sorbet.

INGREDIENTS *2½ cups water* ‖ *3 lemongrass stalks, each 7–8 inches long, cut into 4–5 pieces and bruised* ‖ *½ cup packed brown sugar* ‖ *½ teaspoon grated lime rind* ‖ *⅔ cup lime juice*

ONE Boil the water, lemongrass, and sugar in a saucepan over medium heat for 8–10 minutes or until the sugar has dissolved. **TWO** Strain the syrup and discard the lemongrass solids. Add the lime rind and juice. Set aside until cool. **THREE** Pour the mixture into a freezer box or other container and freeze for 1½ hours or until half-frozen. Take the mixture out of the freezer and blend in a food processor. Return to the container. Whisk at least twice during freezing time. There should be plenty of air whipped into it or it will be too icy and hard. Cover and freeze completely.

Serves 4–6

NUTRIENT ANALYSIS PER SERVING 539 kJ – 127 cal – 0 g protein – 33 g carbohydrate – 33 g sugars – 0 g fat – 0 g saturated fat – 0 g fiber – trace sodium

HEALTHY TIP Limes contain a lot of vitamin C. As early as the eighteenth century, lime juice was found to cure scurvy in sailors who did not have access to fresh fruits or vegetables after many weeks at sea.

Quail eggs in ginger syrup

Quail eggs, a delicacy in Asia, make delicious appetizers and desserts. In this dish they are served with a delicious ginger syrup, an unusual but delightful combination.

INGREDIENTS *24 quail eggs* ‖ *2½ cups water* ‖ *⅓ cup packed brown sugar* ‖ *1 inch fresh ginger root, peeled and thinly sliced*

ONE Gently break the eggs one by one into a bowl and discard the shells. **TWO** Boil the water, sugar, and ginger in a saucepan until the sugar has dissolved. **THREE** Add the quail eggs and cook for 1–2 minutes until the yolks are half-cooked. Spoon the quail eggs and syrup into individual bowls (leaving the sliced ginger in the pan) and serve hot.

Serves 4 as a dessert

NUTRIENT ANALYSIS PER SERVING 800 kJ – 190 cal – 10 g protein – 20 g carbohydrate – 20 g sugars – 8 g fat – 2 g saturated fat – 0 g fiber – 200 mg sodium

HEALTHY TIP Eggs are the cheapest source of high-quality protein. They contain vitamin D, which aids in the absorption of calcium and phosphorus, essential for keeping bones strong.

Sticky rice with mango

This is one of the best known of all Thai desserts. In Thailand, the mango season comes in April, when there are many varieties available in the stores; some taste better when they are green, crisp, and crunchy, others when they are fully ripe.

INGREDIENTS *1¼ cups white sticky rice* ‖ *½ cup coconut milk* ‖ *¼ cup water* ‖ *2 tablespoons palm or coconut sugar* ‖ *½ teaspoon salt (optional)* ‖ *4 ripe mangoes*

ONE Soak the rice in a bowl of water for at least 3 hours. **TWO** Drain the rice and transfer to a steamer basket lined with a double thickness of cheesecloth. Spread the rice in the steamer. **THREE** Bring the water to a rolling boil. Taking care not to burn your hand, set the steamer basket over the water, reduce heat, cover, and steam for 20–25 minutes or until the rice swells and is glistening and tender. Check and replenish the water every 10 minutes or so. **FOUR** Mix the coconut milk, measured water, and sugar in a small saucepan and stir over low heat until sugar has dissolved. **FIVE** As soon as the rice is cooked, spoon it into a bowl, mix with the coconut milk mixture, cover, and let rest for 10 minutes. **SIX** Peel the mangoes and slice off the outside cheeks of each, removing as much flesh as you can in large pieces. Avoid cutting very close to the pit, where the flesh is fibrous. Discard the pit. Slice each piece of mango into 4–5 pieces lengthwise, arrange on a serving plate, and serve with a side portion of sticky rice with coconut milk.

Serves 4 as a dessert

NUTRIENT ANALYSIS PER SERVING 1687 kJ – 400 cal – 7 g protein – 80 g carbohydrate – 34 g sugars – 6 g fat – 3 g saturated fat – 4 g fiber – 35 mg sodium

HEALTHY TIP Mangoes contain an enzyme similar to papain in papayas, which acts as a digestive aid. They are high in fiber, low in calories and sodium, rich in vitamin A, and are a good source of vitamins B and C as well as potassium, calcium, and iron.

Sago pudding with white lotus seeds

Sago palms (or, strictly speaking, cycads) grow profusely in Thailand, and their trunks provide a host for orchids. Sago pudding is a traditional Thai dessert, made from starch extracted from the pith of the sago palm. Lotus seeds are removed from the flowers and dried in the sun. They are widely available in Thai and Asian supermarkets, but if you cannot find them, use fresh young coconut in this recipe instead.

INGREDIENTS *1 oz white lotus seeds* ‖ *⅔ cup unsweetened coconut milk, well stirred, or milk* ‖ *1½ teaspoons all-purpose flour* ‖ *¼ teaspoon salt* ‖ *2 cups water* ‖ *½ cup sago or tapioca* ‖ *¼ cup baker's or superfine sugar*

ONE Soak the lotus seeds in boiling water for 30 minutes and drain. **TWO** In a small saucepan, mix together the coconut milk or milk, flour, and salt and cook over medium heat for 2–3 minutes or until slightly thickened. Transfer to a small bowl and set aside. **THREE** Boil the water with the lotus seeds briskly in a medium-sized saucepan. Add the sago and stir with a wooden spoon for a few minutes over medium heat. Keep stirring until the grains are swollen, clear, and shiny. Reduce the heat if necessary. **FOUR** Add the sugar and stir until it has dissolved. The sago and lotus seeds should now be almost cooked. **FIVE** Let the sago pudding thicken for 10 minutes; serve in individual bowls with a few spoonfuls of coconut cream on top. Serve warm.

Serves 4 as a dessert

NUTRIENT ANALYSIS PER SERVING 1135 kJ – 270 cal – 3 g protein – 47 g carbohydrate – 14 g sugars – 9 g fat – 4 g saturated fat – 0 g fiber – 165 mg sodium

HEALTHY TIP Lotus seeds are a mild sedative, helpful in calming the mind. They are rich in a repair enzyme that protects the plant from damage. Scientists have grown lotus plants from seeds that were more than 1,000 years old.

Fresh fruit platter

There is an abundance of fresh fruit in Thailand, especially pineapples, which are grown between rubber trees on huge plantations and are great to eat after seafood. Papaya is one of the most delicious of all tropical fruits, and watermelon is always refreshing on a hot summer day.

INGREDIENTS *1 fresh pineapple, ripe and yellow* ‖ *¼ watermelon, sweet and red* ‖ *1 small papaya, ripe and slightly orange* ‖ *½ lime*

ONE Use a large, sharp knife to chop off the crown and tail of the pineapple, then slice it vertically into quarters. Cut out the flesh, leaving enough of the outside shell to give a smooth underside, free of indentations. Discard the skin. Cut out the hard core from each quarter. **TWO** Put the pineapple on a large platter and cut it laterally into slices about ½ inch thick. Push the slices alternately ½ inch to the left and right to show that they are separate. **THREE** Slice the watermelon lengthwise into two long pieces. Cut out the flesh and discard the rind. Arrange it next to the pineapple on the platter and slice it across in a similar way. **FOUR** Peel the papaya, discard the skin, and slice it in quarters lengthwise. Carefully scoop out the seeds from each quarter with a spoon, then use a sharp knife to pare away any remaining white seed lining. **FIVE** Place the quarters on the platter, make vertical cuts as before, and arrange the pieces in a similar way. **SIX** Place the lime next to the papaya. Leave the fruit platter in the refrigerator for at least 20 minutes to chill. Squeeze the lime juice over the papaya when serving.

Serves 4–6

NUTRIENT ANALYSIS PER SERVING 724 kJ – 170 cal – 2 g protein – 40 g carbohydrate – 27 g sugars – 1 g fat – 0 g saturated fat – 2 g fiber – 12 mg sodium

HEALTHY TIP Fresh fruits contain more healing properties than canned fruit. Pineapple is a good example, being rich in the enzyme bromelain (a natural anti-inflammatory agent), which is destroyed by the heat used in the canning process.

Black sticky rice with egg custard

Many different toppings are available in Thailand with this traditional dessert. Wrapped in a banana leaf, it was once served at breakfast with tea or coffee but is now eaten at any time of the day.

INGREDIENTS *1¼ cups black sticky rice* ‖ *½ cup coconut milk* ‖ *¼ cup water* ‖ *2 tablespoons palm or coconut sugar*

EGG CUSTARD *⅓ cup coconut milk* ‖ *5 large eggs* ‖ *1¼ cups coconut or palm sugar, cut into small pieces if hard* ‖ *1 teaspoon vanilla extract*

ONE Soak the rice in a bowl of water overnight. **TWO** Fill a wok or steamer pan with water. Place in the bamboo steamer basket or steamer rack, cover, and bring the water to a boil over medium heat. **THREE** Meanwhile, make the egg custard. Mix together the coconut milk, eggs, sugar, and vanilla extract until the sugar has dissolved. **FOUR** Pour the custard through a strainer into a steamer bowl until it is three-quarters full. **FIVE** Taking care not to burn your hand, set the custard bowl inside the steamer basket, simmer for 10–15 minutes or until set around the edges, and set aside. Let stand at room temperature for about 30 minutes or until set. **SIX** Drain and spread the rice into the same bamboo steamer basket over a double thickness of cheesecloth. Cover and simmer for 30–35 minutes or until the rice swells and is glistening and tender. Check and replenish the water every 10 minutes or so. **SEVEN** Mix the coconut milk and sugar in a small saucepan and stir over low heat until the sugar has dissolved. **EIGHT** As soon as the rice has cooked, spoon it into a bowl. Mix in the coconut milk mixture, cover, and set aside for 10 minutes. Serve the black sticky rice on a small dessert plate and spoon the egg custard over the top.

Serves 4 as a dessert

NUTRIENT ANALYSIS PER SERVING 2877 kJ – 684 cal – 15 g protein – 123 g carbohydrate – 77 g sugars – 16 g fat – 7 g saturated fat – 1 g fiber – 150 mg sodium

HEALTHY TIP Although it's sometimes called glutinous rice, sticky rice is gluten-free. In black sticky rice, a layer of bran covers the rice grains. Rice bran contains twice as much fiber as oat bran.

Index

Acknowledgments

I would like to thank everyone at Hamlyn who was involved with this project and helped to make it a success. I am grateful to my friends Rawipim Paijit ("Numwan"), Benjavan Kidhadamrongdet ("Ben"), and Chantra Robinson for their help and encouragement. My thanks are especially due to my partner John Lewell who has helped me with expressing my ideas and to our son Jonathan for his willingness to taste new dishes.

EXECUTIVE EDITOR Nicky Hill
EDITOR Charlotte Wilson
DEPUTY CREATIVE DIRECTOR AND DESIGN Geoff Fennell
PHOTOGRAPHY William Reavell
FOOD STYLIST Tonia George
PROP STYLIST Liz Hippisley
SENIOR PRODUCTION CONTROLLER Manjit Sihra